THE ACHIEVER EFFECT

LORENZO SELLERS

Text copyright©2013 Lorenzo Sellers

All Rights Reserved

To my dearly departed grandmother for believing in my talents as a writer

PREFACE

I wrote this book with one thing in mind… to open people's minds to receive their own inner wealth and potential. My whole life I have always been interested in helping many different people achieve their goals and dreams. The satisfaction of the people I helped succeed always brought me great joy.

This book shares information on how to "improve" your life in multitudes and give you an entirely new view on how things can work for you within your own life. You will learn in this book how to completely open your mind and receive new concepts, ideas, point of views that *can* and *will* change your direction in life. Within part II of this book, you will also learn how to walk the path of the successful and learn how to use your open mind to win.

I want to thank my mother above all people for motivating me in writing this book. I wouldn't have realized that my way of thinking was different.

I also want to thank the motivational speakers and influential people that really reached out to me with their words which helped me realize that motivating and inspiring people was something that I was born to do. People like:

Les Brown

Zig Ziglar

Jack Canfield

Will Smith

Martin Luther King Jr.

Brian Tracy

I would like to thank one more person. I would like to thank my grandmother Ellen Williams who passed when I was still in 5th

Grade. She always believed in my kind heart and passion in writing. I miss you every day and this book is dedicated to you.

Lorenzo L.
Sellers, 2013

TABLE OF CONTENTS

Part I: Opening a Closed Mind

CHAPTER ONE:

LOOKING WITHIN SELF..2

CHAPTER TWO:

OPEN UP! I WANT TO COME IN! 8

CHAPTER THREE:

SEVEN LOCKS OF THE CLOSED MIND..16

CHAPTER FOUR:

UNLOCKING A CLOSED MIND: POSITIVE ATTITUDE (KEY OF POSITIVITY)..36

CHAPTER FIVE:

UNLOCKING A CLOSED MIND: IMAGINE THAT! (KEY OF IMAGINATION)..50

CHAPTER SIX:

UNLOCKING A CLOSED MIND: WHAT ARE YOUR DREAMS? (KEY OF DREAMS).......................................60

CHAPTER SEVEN:

UNLOCKING A CLOSED MIND: BE PASSIONATE! (KEY OF PASSION)... 70

CHAPTER EIGHT:

UNLOCKING A CLOSED MIND: BEING OPTIMISTIC (KEY OF OPTIMISM)...78

CHAPTER NINE:

UNLOCKING A CLOSED MIND: WHAT YOU DO HAVE (KEY OF GRATITUDE)...86

CHAPTER TEN:

UNLOCKING A CLOSED MIND: GROW AND FLOURISH (KEY OF LOVE)...96

CHAPTER ELEVEN:

SURPASSING YOUR LIMITATIONS: ROAD TO RICHES AND WEALTH..105

CHAPTER TWELVE:

THE SECRET TO A JOYFUL AND ABUNDANT LIFE..121

Part II: Walking the Path

CHAPTER THIRTEEN:

WHAT IT MEANS TO DISCOVER YOUR DREAM..134

CHAPTER FOURTEEN:

WHO YOU ARE..144

CHAPTER FIFTEEN:

COMFORT ZONE...152

CHAPTER SIXTEEN:

FAITH IN YOUR DREAM....................................166

CHAPTER SEVENTEEN:

CREATING THE HABIT....................................176

CHAPTER EIGHTEEN:

TIME: A WASTED FACTOR............................190

CHAPTER NINETEEN:

PLAN ON THE MASTERMIND.........................198

CHAPTER TWENTY:

STANDING OUT AND BEING SEEN................ 204

Part I: Opening a Closed Mind

"It doesn't matter when I believe the opportunity will show up. What does matter is what I do when opportunity presents itself"

CHAPTER ONE
Looking Within Self

Your thoughts really do have unimaginable power behind them. They come from a source deep within yourself that controls your actions and the way you live your life right now. It is said *one must know thyself before one can master his or her own universe.*

What is our purpose here on earth? That question always seems to arise within our minds. So we look for the answer in places that we shouldn't be looking. We tend to look for it in other people, religion, books, and

The **ACHIEVER** Effect

videos. The one place that we will always find that answer is within ourselves.

Your purpose is what you create *literally*! Take the time out to think to yourself and ask: *"What am I truly good at doing"?* You truly have something within you that only you can bring to the table of life. We were all born with greatness within us. Problem is, only a few people actually answered the call of greatness that was within them. They changed how the world operated completely. One of the main reasons most of us don't *"pick up the phone"*, lies in our fear of failure or the fear of what other people may think. Those reasons alone hold so many of us back from doing what we really want to do.

Fear is taught to us growing up from infancy. We weren't born with it and society teaches us to implant it into our lives. So what do most people do? We limit ourselves to other people's expectations based off of fear of judgment and hoping for acceptance from what we all call society. Most people literally live their lives according to what others want. Truth be told, that's not what we

The **ACHIEVER** Effect

were created for. No human was ever meant to live their lives off of the expectations of others. We fail to look within ourselves for our true calling.

There is a man today who embraced his inner calling and achieved great things by creating the world's largest computer software, *Microsoft*. Yes, I'm referring to *Bill Gates*. Many people downed his idea and passion for creativity. But Gates chose to listen to his inner voice and continue with his venture. Gates and his business partner Paul Allen had set out to revolutionize the world. Now Gates sits at the top as one of the richest men in the world.

Success for you is only a thought away. If you can conceive it, you can achieve it. Self-doubt created by others around you is the number one culprit to killing your dreams, hopes, and desires. In some cases, it is also created by situations we are placed in. At times, it is really hard to see a "way out" when things aren't going the way you would like them to go.

The **ACHIEVER** Effect

Those are usually the times when life is telling you that you are seriously off track of your calling. Life can be a cruel teacher and the lessons, at times, can be brutal. The response to these lessons can cause the human mind to seriously shut down and lock up resulting in a *closed mind*. Having this type of mind set will close the door to your inner being, making it hard to hear the calling.

This is what causes our imagination to eventually fade into darkness. This has an effect on many parts of your life causing one to become a "robot" in society. This means that you move with the crowd doing the same mundane activity every day without thought. I will definitely touch more onto the subject of imagination later on in this book.

What happens if you realize that you went off track and want to better your situation? A lot of people look toward a higher being for an answer for all their problems. They ask for ways out, but refuse to move into action when they get that nudge. That nudge represents your inner self trying to break through. But sadly, a lot people expect to get everything for nothing in return. When I was a child, I was taught that God will only meet you half way. But you must put in the work to meet Him.

Self-awareness is a great factor and the main point in this chapter. You must be aware of your own gifts and talents before you can truly begin to live life the way you want to live it. We do live in the land of opportunity. The same wind blows on us all. This means that the same chance to living a full and happy life is within us all. Call this your starting line. This is your life. Life isn't lived by what you're supposed to do, but by what you want to do.

"Plant a seed of desire in your mind. Water it with faith, love, and action. Now watch it grow into a mighty tree of accomplishment"- Lorenzo L. Sellers

CHAPTER TWO
Open Up! I Want To Come In!

Well, here we are. Your guests have arrived and the opportunity, ideas, inspirations, love, success, luck, and any other great thing that can possibly happen to you. Those with open minds can receive all these amazing things and more. The main reason why these people can receive these great things is because they mentally choose to keep their "door" wide open.

The **ACHIEVER** Effect

In other words, they possess an open mind. This means they can see different perspectives in any situation. They can truly find the good in everything. This means they have a positive attitude about it. I will go into deeper detail about positivity in chapter 4.

There are many historical men and women who kept an open mind about most factors in their life and did great things with their lives. I was once told that our mind is like a parachute, it only works when it's open. To be fair, it's perfectly understandable why it is hard for most people to open their minds to new concepts and ideas. Somewhere, somehow, a standard has been set for how people are "supposed" to live their lives. We have been divided into categories and classes. The rich or wealthy are the highest of the social classes. They live their life with a tremendous amount of options. Then you have the middle class. Still have quite a few options on how to live their lives, but not as much as the wealthy. Finally, you have the poor or poverty class. It is said that those who live in this class have little to no options and cannot escape this lifestyle.

I truly believe that this is false. Your entire life setting, no matter what it may be, can be changed with a single thought or idea. It doesn't matter where you were born and who gave birth to you. Your life literally revolves around you and your state of mind. Granted, it's difficult to have an open mind when you are surrounded with close minded individuals.

Those are the main ones who will put down any and all ideas that will inspire you to go out and do great things. It's has a similar effect that of chains holding you down in place. However, those chains can be as real as you want them to be. This is why this book encourages opening the mind to see your inner "key". *You are what you surround yourself with.*

Here is a set of questions for you that will gauge where you are mentally when it comes to having an open mind at this point in your life. It is best you be honest with yourself.

That way, you will have more of an accurate result. Write these questions down in your notepad somewhere and keep it with you.

Self-Check Mindset Questions

1. Am I doing what I really want to do at this point in my life? If no, explain why.

2. Do I get slightly irritated when I hear someone else I know is doing what they want and achieving their goals?

3. Am I putting myself down whenever I feel like I have an idea that can change the world?

4. Are my goals I set out to do being met at this point?

5. Do I believe that my goals are too big to achieve?

6. Whenever I hear of legit opportunities to make more money, do I jump right to skepticism because I don't believe it or I heard that anything else besides having a job is false?

The **ACHIEVER** Effect

7. Do I believe that success only comes to those "born" with the opportunity?

8. Do I feel trapped within the "box" set by society?

9. Am I truly happy with my life right now?

10. Do I appreciate the things and people I already have in my life?

The result of this test is completely dependent upon you. If you answered yes to most of these, you might have a closed mind and self-doubt. But fear not!!! That's exactly what this book is for. The goals of this book it to open up your mind to different perspectives in life and help you achieve enlightenment.

You must be hungry for self-development. Most people live their lives like a closed rose. It isn't' until you open your mind that you blossom into a beautiful and radiant flower. Some people find comfort being negative about some things in life because it "justifies" why they aren't following their dreams. This mindset is simply unhealthy!!!

The **ACHIEVER** Effect

You have people out there dying of broken hearts because they did the opposite of what they wanted to do. A quote from one of *Les Brown's* seminars states that *"most heart failures occur on a Monday morning between 8:00am and 9:00am"*.

People are dying from the thought of going to work!!! Granted, some people out there love their jobs because they can see the good in what they do. That goes with having an open mind. But you do have people out there who would rather be following their own personal goals and desires. But because of whatever they heard their entire life about how life works; they close their minds to infinite possibilities. Those are usually the ones dying of a broken heart.

So in short, having a closed mind can literally kill you. Not just physically, but also spiritually as well. This book will alter a closed minded person's life and place them back on track. I cannot express enough how vital that changing your mindset for a closed to open position is to your health. One of these issues, for example, goes into weight loss or muscle gain. We hear it all the time, "I can't lose weight because…" or "I can't gain muscle or look that way because…."

The "can't" is a product of fear which represents a lock on your mind that prevents your "inner door" to fully open. I will explain this in the next chapter. Simply put, your success is right outside the door. No matter how big your success may be, it will be able to come into your life only if you allow it to. There is no such thing as "I can't be successful". You can and you will be. Now you are ensuring it by reading this book. You are one of the few who decided to take your own fate, destiny, future into your own hands. Life is exactly what you make it. And in the rest of this "mind bible", you will discover, for those who haven't discovered it yet, your true full potential. Let's begin!!!

"Your mind is like a parachute. It only works if it is open". - Anthony J. D´Angelo

CHAPTER THREE
Seven Locks of the Closed Mind

In this chapter, we will be going over the seven emotions that will completely close your mind to any concept or idea that may better one's life. Keep in mind, there are other factors that contribute to a closed mind. But in this book, I will discuss only seven *BIG* emotions, which I like to call, the seven locks of the closed mind.

These "locks" serves a means to lock out any kind of succession in your life. It causes a hindrance to a career, goal, job, venture, or any other desire you want out of life. Who creates these locks in life? It is usually created by the people who deal with this interference. In most cases however, it may be the people you choose to surround yourself with. You are who you hang around with.

So if you choose to stick around negative people all the time, then that's exactly the type of person you become and circumstances that may be involved are also negative. Also, on the other side of that coin, surround yourself with positive and successful people and that's how you and your life will tend to turn out. More opportunities tend to arise and you live a much happier life. So stew within the negative and watch out, here comes the locks!!!

ANGER

Whew!!! Watch out for this one! This emotion is the first lock that will definitely slam the door shut in your mind. Have you ever gotten into an argument and completely stopped listening to what the other party has to say? You are no longer in taking information but only spitting or yelling it out. You refuse to see the other person's angle on the subject at hand and cannot come to a peaceful resolution.

This goes for anything situation in your life. If something you don't like happens to in your life, anger is usually the first emotion we reach for. *For example, you are working at a corporation and you apply for a position. But you weren't the only one who applied for it. There may be one other who wants that promotion. As time goes by, you are working 110 percent to insure that you get that promotion over the other person. The upper management made their decision and you find out that you were not selected for the position.* This is outrageous!!! You worked twice as hard as anyone at the company and they still gave the promotion to another person. Some people may react differently. But in most cases, anger is the first reaction and causes one to perform actions not very favorable to say the least.

So instead of accepting it and considering why they chose another, many people tend to complain about it or worse, quit. If one keeps complaining or quits just because things didn't go their way that one time, how can you expect to achieve your goals. Life is full of setbacks and disappointments, but anger will cause you to accept a temporary "defeat" and close your mind to other ways to approach your goal.

PRIDE

The second lock on the door of a closed mind. I would say this one is worse than anger. Pride for many centuries has cause downfalls of kingdoms. So imagine what it does to a single person. Pride blinds you to see any other concept or idea that differs from you own. This brings the true meaning to having a closed mind. Heck, it makes it air tight!

The **ACHIEVER** Effect

This lock prevents progress in every sense of the word. It compares to you hitting a brick wall. Pride is harder to get over than anger. Anger subsides after a while; Pride weaves into your beliefs, right or wrong. So this barrier will definitely be a little harder to get over. This lock on a closed mind will end relationships, partnerships, friendships, and any alliance that you may have as long as their concepts contradicts yours.

It is said that pride is a sin in many religious aspects. Quite believable if you notice the effect it has on your life. Nothing good comes from it at all. Let's go over the list of effects this barrier has on your life:

- Prevents progress
- Ends every type of relationship
- Creates hostility (at times)
- Blocks different views from entering the mind
- Potential isolation

The **ACHIEVER** Effect

As you can see, pride will indeed ruin your life. Pride is created through low self-esteem of one's self. So you create it to make yourself feel superior to others. So ideas coming from anyone else will not get your "seal of approval". This effect some company leaders who allows pride to reign. His or her company may never grow with that type of mind set. A leader who is open to all, gains the wisdom of all. Although anger will close and lock the door temporarily, pride follows shortly after to keep it air tight shut. But this lock is all but indestructible. There is hope for those with pride running through them. We will discuss the key to unlocking this barrier in later chapters.

RESENTMENT

There will always be circumstances that take place within our lives that will be, to say the least, undesirable. But you can both accept it and move on or you can stew in the hate. In many cases, some people blame the government for their financial problems. So they start to resent everything preventing them from moving on or growing from the circumstance that has taken place.

At this point, it would be hard for anyone to see the party being blamed any other way. There are a lot of great opportunities that this country of ours provides. But even resentment can hold us back from truly seeing them. For example, *ever since you were a child, all you heard from your parents was, "rich people are people who cheated and tricked other people to get where they are". So they resented anyone who is even remotely successful in areas they weren't.*

Sad thing is, people inherit these views from their parents. So you have a lot of people who prevent themselves from seeing any other view simply because that's all they ever heard. So the kids grow up to resent the "cause" of their parent's pain. This way of thinking will definitely create a closed mind because you only see things in one point in view. This lock up in your mind usually follows after anger, the first lock.

The **ACHIEVER** Effect

These emotions that make you feel bad have a seriously negative impact in your life and your experiences will usually follow suit. The more you resent anything, the more it continues on "doing" what you resented it for in the first place. This is definitely one of the most devastating locks on the door of a closed mind.

You simply don't profit from this what so ever. It's a poison that will cut your life in half. Meaning you will only see the bad side of life rather than the good because you are concentrating all your energy on what is bad. It's best to see everything in different perspectives to get a good idea on how things work. Resentment creates limits or barriers for you and that is truly last thing you want. Expansion of the mind is prevented through resentment. When you expand your mind, you create more room for success in your life to settle down. However, this lock up will take up space in your own personal "universe", and create nothing but problems for you. But like many things, this road block is possible to overcome depending on how long you been exposed to resentment. Once this lock is gone, an entirely new world will be opened up for you. One where you can see advantages and opportunities as clear as day!

FEAR

Fear of the unknown can be a little scary to those who don't travel outside their comfort zone very often. It holds you back from taking risks and exploring areas you never thought about tapping into. Fear is the fourth lock to a closed mind. This concept closes a mind faster than other emotion there is. Have you ever heard the quote, "*I don't see because I choose not to see*"? Fear contributes to that quote. In terms of the mind, fear is undesirable change that takes place within your life. This causes one to act out anger, pride, and you guessed it once again, resentment! One example goes back to the old ages when witches were running about. Hundreds of people accused of being "different" was burned, drowned, and tortured for years by angry mobs. Why they were angry you ask? *Fear*. It was the fear of the unknown, the unfamiliar, that drove them. Because of their unwillingness to learn more about the witches, a lot of people died.

Did you catch the lesson within that story? We all know by now that having a closed mind can be fatal to your success, but a group of people with a closed mind with the sole purpose of destroying what they fear or don't understand can be fatal period! This emotion caused wars, fights, and many violent acts all together. This severely limits your capability of understanding a concept or idea that may change the way you think, or change your life in general.

Another example would be the story of Jesus. *Jesus was changing lives every day as he traveled spreading the word of God and performing miracles. He brought hope to many lives within his lifetime, but the government and other people in power feared that this will bring undesirable change. So they organized to put Jesus to death.* Fear causes a short sight, meaning one won't be able to see a bigger picture. It also causes one to create reasons why they won't leave their comfort zone. And to them, their reasons are justifiable. The acronym to fear is "False Evidence Appearing Real".

That "false evidence" was created by their mind saturated in fear. It made them feel as though what Jesus was doing was an evil act because it went against everything they believed in. I describe fear as a box that surrounds you. The walls are close and it's hard for you to move around. But a lot of people choose to stay within that box simply because it is what they are used to. It's a familiar territory to them and they like knowing exactly what comes next. I am here to tell you that just because it's familiar don't mean that it's the best way to go.

Many successful people braved their fears and traveled to unfamiliar territories because they realized the truth behind what fear really is. Sounds like a simple task right? For many, getting over this barrier takes a lot of work and the right motivation.

JEALOUSY

The **ACHIEVER** Effect

Jealousy brings with it the *"legendary green eyed monster"*. The term "monster" is well deserved considering that jealousy destroys any hope from you being truly successful. It's no secret that there are a ton of people out there who achieved exactly what they want to do in life. That they are truly living life the way they see fit. And with those types of people out there, you have people who look upon the successful with envy. So what do they do? They do absolutely nothing at all to help themselves achieve their wants and desires. At this point, this group of individuals feels bad and places their mind in a state where they lack motivation to do what they what out of life.

Instead of borrowing strength from the successful, they complain how their life is different and name all the situations and circumstances that may have happened to them to succeed. A wise man once told me *if there is someone out there who, by chance, is doing something that you would like to do and are successful, then it would be wise to take notes and learn from them.* Jealousy would only get in the way of taking in knowledge and wisdom. People who embrace jealousy also enjoy bringing other people down who has already achieved an open mind and has a desire to want more out of life. It is like that old but true saying, *"misery loves company"*. Say, for example, *that you and your friend grew up together. You and they know each other as though you were siblings and shared each other's dreams. You both get jobs as adults and eventually forget about what your dreams were. Then one day, you decide that you want to go after your dreams and make them a reality. So you start to get to work and you are doing really well. Now your friend however is still doing the same ole routine day after day. They see you doing well, and instead of borrowing from your strength, they try to bring you back down on the level that they are at.*

Jealousy even has a way of ending friendships as well! This monster of an emotion can be beaten however. Later on in this book, you will learn how to slay this beast and win the day!

The **ACHIEVER** Effect

HOPELESSNESS

This lock of the closed mind is by far the worst I believe. There is nothing worse than not having any kind of hope of living the life you want. With this emotion, you tend to feel drained most of your days. It feels as though there is no fire, no passion, and no motivation at all to live. This emotion is usually caused by an event that may have taken place that took or "stole" your hope away.

Your mind is closed off to believe that there is cause to keep going. Without a sound basis of belief, one may find themselves lost in the darkness of the hopeless. There are many examples by which I can explain the effects of hopelessness such as, job termination, death in the family, relationship problems, debt, abundance of bills, etc. that may create the "in the hole" feeling as if there is no way you can get out. This takes its toll on your mind as it strips away any ideas to better your situation.

Another way to describe hopelessness is depression. Your inner spirit will fill up with negativity and eventually cause a negative attitude and mindset. Yes, it's all about the mindset! You have a lot of people in the world today who believe that their problems are bigger than they are. So they go into the mindset of, and you guessed it, hopelessness. Now that this effect has kicked in, they will find it very hard to find a solution to their problems or to "see the light at the end of the tunnel". This creates something toward the effect of a maze in your mind. Can you imagine walking around for days, weeks, years to find the fastest way to the exit? Just thinking about it makes you believe that it is hopeless.

Hopelessness prevents the human mind to think outside the box, hindering your progress. For example, let's say that you are overweight and you are desperately trying to lose a lot of weight and every day you see people walking around happy, healthy, and slim or fit. Two things happen at this point. Either you say that you will look better than that soon or you could say that you will never look that way or even remotely close. A lot of people, believe it or not, actually choose the second thought as their primary one.

And now, they fell into the mindset of complete hopelessness. They now have little to no motivation to go on to realize their dream of a fit body. One must get over this barrier to fully realize their dream.

ARROGANCE

This can be mistaken for self-confidence. Arrogance plays a big part as the final lock on a closed mind. It tricks the mind into believing that it knows everything it needs to know about, well, everything. It completely blinds you to the fact that there may be new information about everything. Being arrogant, you refuse to believe that there is nobody who knows more than you on any given subject. So in turn, receiving new ideas or concepts from other people is simply out of the question.

Arrogance is usually attained when a person has a little success in life. To my experience, basketball players show an excessive amount of this trait. To some of them, there is no one in existence who can be better at the sport than them. Keeping an open mind that there are better players out there is hard for the arrogant. So it is hard for them to expand and grow as a player and a person. But let's not put this trait only on basketball players. This barrier lies within us all and has the potential to grow unless we allow it.

Arrogance on comes when we allow our self-confidence to overflow. I'm not saying it isn't ok to be confident in your abilities and yourself. Like my elders always told me when I was younger, "don't let it go to your head". The effects that this trait has on your life could be damaging. You could lose relationships with your friends, weaken it with family, and cause all kinds of hang ups in life as well. It also causes your perspective to be a little skewed. This is definitely a "one way street". Your mind only believes in a one way conversation. Your way or no way!

These locks within a closed mind can make it hard to open the door. As children we were born with open minds. We were always

The **ACHIEVER** Effect

curious and wanting to try new things. As we go through life, these locks are created through our own experiences. What determines if we wind up with an open or closed mind depends on what we take out of these experiences. This book is to help with those who might have taken a "wrong turn" and closed their minds. The mission is to help you as the readers enter a state of mind that will help you receive the abundance of life and opportunity so you can turn that into your own personal success. And even if you already have an open mind, you might pick up something new within this book you wouldn't have thought about before. We all learn and grow with new concepts entered within our lives. Now let us begin our journey to opening your mind and speeding up your success story to come!

"Our deepest fear is not that we are inadequate. Our deepest fear is that we are powerful beyond measure. It is our light, not our darkness that most frightens us. We ask ourselves, 'Who am I to be brilliant, gorgeous, talented, and fabulous?' Actually, who are you not to be? You are a child of God. Your playing small does not serve the world. There is nothing enlightened about shrinking so that other people won't feel insecure around you. We are all meant to shine, as children do. We were born to make manifest

the glory of God that is within us. It's not just in some of us; it's in everyone. And as we let our own light shine, we unconsciously give other people permission to do the same. As we are liberated from our own fear, our presence automatically liberates others."- Marianne Williamson

CHAPTER FOUR

Unlocking a Closed Mind:

Positive Attitude (Key of Positivity)

Starting off by being positive can and will open doors for you within your life. It can change your perspective on any given situation giving you insight to the whole picture. Granted, it's difficult to have this mindset all the time, but I can assure you it is entirely possible. Positivity can put you at a mindset where you can see things more clearly. This also introduces enthusiasm which helps make things easier to accomplish. We all been in unfavorable situations where having a negative attitude seems to be the ideal way of dealing. Negativity can spiritually and physically drain you. So not only are you still feeling bad, but you cannot see any other way of improving the set situation you may be in.

Having a positive attitude is the only key choice here to clearing the way. This concept also helps out when you want to "think outside the box". Holding and believing in this concept will inspire and open your mind to the different possibilities out there in the world. You begin to see that life is a magnificent ride and opportunities tend to come to you as easily as water flows downstream in a river. We call people who we witnessed going through that experience the "lucky" ones. Luck has little to do with their abundance of good fortune. They understand that having a positive attitude yields positive results. You attract what you literally put out. Have you ever noticed that those who complain the most about everything tend to stay in that situation? Sit back and meditate on that for a little. They resist their situation and it keeps coming back for more. It was Carl Jung who once quoted, "what you resist persists". Truer words have never been spoken. Negativity is a resisting factor and causes all sorts of havoc on your life.

It impedes on your progress and expansion of your mind. All things begin with a single thought. And if you allow negative energy to dominate that thought, negative circumstances pop up out of nowhere. This is what creates bad days or "bad luck". I'm not implying that bad situations don't happen to those with a positive mindset. What I am saying is that it is completely up to you if that negative situation grows into something more or it dies before it has a chance to grow at all.

When I put on my uniform every night before I go to work, I look at myself in the mirror and begin to tell myself not to let anything put me in a bad mood. This is my day and it is completely up to me how it turns out from here. I even say a verse from Psalms 23:4. *"Yea though I walk through the valley of the Shadow of Death, I will fear no evil; for thou art with me; thy rod and thy staff they comfort me"*. It's not the verse itself that spurs me on but the meaning behind the words.

I will not let negative people or situations get to me and dominate my thoughts. I shall keep an open mind and stay positive. And usually my day goes by very quickly. It is all in your attitude. Let's dig more into advantages and pitfalls of having attitude. When most people hear the word attitude, they think it to be negative at first. But let's remember that there are two types of attitudes out there; positive and negative. You can always tell what type of attitude a person has by reading their body language, listening to the way they speak, or by their actions.

A positive attitude is very contagious. It causes people around you to smile and possibly uplift their day as well. A person

The **ACHIEVER** Effect

with a positive attitude is usually the one with energy and sees no task set as "too big", which mixes with enthusiasm. To my experience, it's a key element needed in any work space to improve teamwork and efficiency. Employers absolutely love the person with a positive attitude. A few qualities that many employers look for is timeliness, cleanliness, and a "can-do" or, as we all know it, positive attitude. It has been proven that one person's good vibes can change the tides of many. This, in many cases, provides a huge money making advantage to employers. But why stop there? If you are self-employed, having a positive attitude consistently could indeed take your income ratio to great heights.

How you may ask? This key element will help you keep an open mind and a look out for any opportunity that may help your self-made business' grow. One man who exemplified the true meaning of being positive created the well popular candy known as Jelly Belly jelly beans. His name was David Klein. He first came up with this

The **ACHIEVER** Effect

idea back in 1976 to create flavored gourmet jelly beans. Today, it's one of America's most favorite candy brands to date. Mr. Klein had a seriously positive attitude about people. He loved seeing people smile as he gave them opportunities to achieve their dreams.

Positivity, as I said before, spreads and opens the minds of many. I believe that from here it is safe to assume that having a negative attitude blocks any good fortune from entering your life.

We will look into how positivity will help affect a person's career in the corporate setting. For example, *Brian has been working for a Big Name corporation for 7 years now. He is constantly early to work and the last to leave at the end of the day. His performance is impeccable and people who he works with really enjoy his presence around the office. Brian's job is really demanding as he handles the financials of the company. But he also takes on other jobs and tasks in different departments to further his thirst for experience. He always shows up with a smile on his face and a song in his heart. If*

The **ACHIEVER** Effect

positivity had a face, it would be Brian's. Evaluations are coming up and this could be the chance he was waiting for to be promoted to the Head Sales Manager that he applied for, but he has competition. Steve has been working there for 9 years. Steve is also early to work every day and one of the last people to take off at the end of the day. His performance is also impeccable in what he does but his attitude drives people away. Steve believes in doing the bare minimum. He works in the sales department of the company and he also applied for the same position as Brian. So as far as sales go, Steve has more experience than Brian does in sales. The CEO and the board of directives look at both the profiles of the two candidates. Who do you think got the promotion? It was a dead lock at first. But they eventually gave the promotion to Brian.

What could have changed the tie into a landslide? Steve had more experience and had seniority over Brian. So why did Brian end up winning the day? The CEO called those who worked with them both and asked

The **ACHIEVER** Effect

who would they follow? Because of Brian's uplifting and positive attitude, it motivated other people to do a little more. He is an inspiration to the office and a valuable asset to the company. One person's good vibes can turn the tide of many. Even though Brian had little to no experience in sales, his enthusiasm gave him the potential of a fast learner. His mind was open to receive new information and expand.

Remember, in the work setting, it's not always the more experienced that gets the promotion. Sometimes, it completely depends on your attitude. It is way easier to work with a positive person than a negative person. The CEO chose to follow the path of least resistance. Most people don't like to be positive simply because they are afraid of what other people think. You do have folks out there who will bash and try to bring down positivity just because they feel like it doesn't have a place around them. But I can guarantee you this; you will make more friends and forge relationships with different people than you will have enemies. This in turn will expose you to many different ideas and concepts that could potentially change your life and in some cases, increase your income flow.

For those with your own businesses or thinking about starting one, this may be a key factor for you. It's no secret that working with two heads yields better results than working with one. Remember, nobody wants to work with a "negative nancy". So having a positive attitude goes a long way in the world of making money. With that being said, the question arises, *how do I stay positive on a daily basis?* I understand that staying positive on a daily basis can be challenging for many. There are factors to consider like, where you live, the people you are around, what your work environment consist of, etc. Well here are some small actions you can do daily to help keep a healthy and positive attitude.

Daily Tips for a Positive Attitude

The **ACHIEVER** Effect

- *Wake up early-* Get a head start on your day. This way, you have time to do everything you need to do before you head in to work or school. So by the time you arrive, you are ready and fully awake to start your day!

- *Read motivating and inspiring books-* One of the best ways to maintain a positive attitude is by reading positive books. These books serve to encourage you, inspire you, and teach you to be positive. This requires that you sit still and focus on the message the book. By focusing on something positive it helps you to keep a positive mindset throughout your day.

- *Listen to podcasts /cds-* This is one of the best ways to maintain a positive attitude. Listen to motivating and inspiring podcasts or cds. The magic behind this is that you can listen to them anywhere. You can listen while you working, driving, exercising, walking, or in flight. Do your best to listen to something positive every day.

- *Exercise-* This is a personal favorite of mine. Exercise will help reduce stress and expel any negative energy you may have built up during the day. By doing this step, you also improve your health which helps to boost your energy. I recommend you perform this step at least 3 times a week. It's a fact that when you look good, you feel good. And feeling good is great!

- *Meditate-* Meditation will provide a somewhat spiritual connection to your inner self. Clear your head of all thoughts and concentrate on what your goals are in life. Leave all negative thoughts out. This method will also help connect you to the "Infinite Intelligence" or to God. Having inner peace leads to an outer peace or a positive attitude.

The **ACHIEVER** Effect

- *Keep the positive around-* One of the best moves you can ever make is to keep positive people around you. The company you keep has a huge impact on your life. These are the people you see on a daily basis and the last thing you need is someone negative constantly being in your ear. If you haven't already, surround yourself with people who you want to be like. If you want to be successful, then surround yourself with successful, positive, uplifting people.

Following these steps daily will definitely help you stay deep within the positivity pool. However, one pitfall to life in general is that everything won't always go according to plan. By this happening, a lot of people tend to fall into a temporary "funk" or depression. One thing to remember is that every plan you make won't always go the way you planned it. Knowing this and accepting it before you plan anything, you are more liable to be flexible. This in turn will help you keep a positive attitude even if things go wrong.

The **ACHIEVER** Effect

You will always have another plan to back up your previous one. There is no such thing as barriers on the road to success, just road bumps. Stay positive and enjoy the ride.

"If you don't like something change it; if you can't change it, change the way you think about it." -Mary Engelbreit

CHAPTER FIVE
Unlocking a Closed Mind:

Imagine That! (Key of Imagination)

When we were infants, there was one thing we developed faster than any other skill. This was our imagination. We were told at some point back in our childhood to never lose it. Those were wise words spoken and words most of us should have followed. But as we got older, little by little, most of us start to lose it. We get so absorbed into the

The **ACHIEVER** Effect

standards that society has set; we believed that imagination was simply not needed. This is a huge misconception.

Let us go into what imagination is before we discuss how it can be beneficial to you in your life now. Imagination is the faculty or action of forming new ideas, or images or concepts of external objects not present to the senses. In other words, without imagination, our society and world could never advance. Think of all the pleasures we have such as cars, trains, planes, elevators, buildings, and every other man made invention we have at our disposal. All this came from someone's faculty or imagination. This is by far the greatest gift given to us by God or the "Infinite Intelligence" at birth. It is the foundation to how you can literally change your life. My kindergarten teacher told me to never lose my imagination for it was the key to unlock my future.

I do believe that the lessons that our first teachers taught us may be the most crucial. Think about this for a spell. 97% of Americans had lost their vision or gateway to their imagination. Only 3% utilized this faculty and acted upon it. Truthfully, the only thing that is holding most people back from fulfilling and living the life they want is fear. As I mentioned back in previous chapters, fear is the reason most people don't reach their full potential.

Think of imagination as a rocket and the financial freedom you desire as the moon. In able to get to the moon, you need that rocket! Without it, you may find it difficult to reach your goal. For example, I think of jobs as cars. You can drive on the same level for lifetime, but if your goal is in space, you will never reach it. It doesn't require you to use your imagination what so ever. I understand society frowns upon people who chose to use their imagination and be creative. Why is this you may ask? Because using this gift given to you may cause you to leave the people you know behind. Or that's the fear that they have.

This concept describes the outside area of the "box" most people stay in. When you hear "think outside the box", what are they

The **ACHIEVER** Effect

really telling you? They're saying use your imagination. Schools in our society today don't teach young adults how to use their imagination anymore. It's all about going to college, getting good grades, and getting a good job. We unconsciously tell our kids not to do what they want but to live off the expectation of others. When you look at some kids playing with a box, what do you see? To you, the adult, you see them just sitting in a box, but to them, their inside a castle, rocket ship, mansion, brand new car, spaceship, etc.

They are in the process of visualizing their wants and desires at that point in their young lives. So to them, it's as real to them as you sitting in your car. But at some point we tell our kids to grow up and put away "childish" things. This, unfortunately, also includes their imagination.

So they grow up forgetting how to visualize and use that imagination given to us at birth to their advantage. This is why this concept is an important step to opening your mind. Imagination allows your mind to conceive ideas and concepts not yet come to past. This is a powerful key element for your future success to come rushing in. Major inventors such as Henry Ford, Ben Franklin, J.P. Knight, George Washington Carver, Madam C.J. Walker, and others understood this concept and transformed something that didn't exist into reality and profited from it too! This "hidden talent" that many of us have within our minds can be brought out through constant use. Remember, what you do not use on a daily basis tend to fade and be forgotten.

By using your imagination, it can make your day much more exciting and interesting. You'll find yourself more motivated and happy. Like I stated before, most adults grow out of their imagination; therefore they think they don't have one. By learning to take control of your imagination and by expanding it, you will be feeling much more calm and carefree. Here are some exercises you can perform to "bring this lost treasure" back up to speed.

The **ACHIEVER** Effect

Keys to Imagining:

- **Think about doing something out of the ordinary when you wake up.** - Say, if you normally don't go to animal shelters, maybe go to the store and buy some dog food and run it up to the local animal shelter.

- **Take a ten minute break during the day to go outside, sit on a bench, and watch people walk by.** - Make up life stories for them. Name them. Make up the reason to why they are at that particular place

- **Pretend you have a super cool superpower that you have to hide from people**. - Imagine what the power is, how you use it, and when you will use it.

- **Rearrange your house or room or living area**. This stimulates your brain because you have to learn how to get used to the new arrangement.

The **ACHIEVER** Effect

- **Set up room or area outside and cover it in cheap white sheets**. - Get some paint and just splash it around. It's a stress relief and fun.

- **Try visualization**.-Visualizing your dream helps to make them happen in reality. Think that you are a better person and visualize that you have achieved something for which you are craving for.

Imagining or visualizing a future where you have already achieved your goals will help you manifest this imagine into reality. Opening this floodgate will provide massive results for you. It's like you are setting a finish line for yourself in your mind. You now know what the results look like. Now it's time to move into action and shift things around to transform that imagine into reality. *Henry Ford did this when he thought up a compact version of the V8 engine. Most people said it wasn't possible to make a smaller version the massive engine, but Mr. Ford and his staff kept at it. And after years*

The **ACHIEVER** Effect

of countless attempts to compact this massive engine, he finally achieved his goal.

His vision has finally manifested into reality. Imagination is a powerful key to unlocking your mind and fulfilling your dream or "destiny". The main sign to know that you are on the right track and that you are using your imagination correctly is simply this; you will enter a certain state of mind of happiness and joy within yourself. You begin to feel hope and you start to believe that your future will be a successful one. However, you may bump into other people who will see this and try to *"bring you back to reality"*. You will hear things like, *"that will never work"* or *"you need to get your head out of the clouds and join us down here on planet earth"*.

If you have people like that in your life, I would highly recommend that you leave them behind and out of your life. Those types of people are called the "Nay Sayers" or "Dream Killers". Many people will tell you that whatever you are imagining or attempting to create is completely

The **ACHIEVER** Effect

"unrealistic". Let the record show that is was unrealistic for metal to fly in the air, to turn on a light by having a switch on the wall, for carriages to move without horses, and to broadcast imagines to a box within your home. So what is the point of being "realistic"? Enable for you to have the absolute best chance of succeeding in using your imagination's full potential; you need to eliminate all negativity from your inner circle.

Having an open mind is more than just being able to receive new ideas and concepts from the world around you. It also means that you are able to create those new ideas and concepts the world just may need in the future. You might hold an idea that may save the lives of many. It's time to dust off your imagination and put it to work. Your future literally depends on this!

"Imagination is everything. It is the preview to life's coming attractions". – Albert Einstein

CHAPTER SIX

Unlocking a Closed Mind:

What are your Dreams? (Key of Dreams)

We all get caught daydreaming at our jobs or in school at times. We imagine that we are traveling to another country, or doing our dream job or profession, or even just sitting on the beach enjoying the view of the ocean on a nice sunny day. What is it that you wish to do? Your dreams are your goals and desires you wish to accomplish. Most of

The ACHIEVER Effect

history's greatest achievers were big dreamers. You have famous poets, artists, philosophers, inventors, etc. who made their mark in this world simply by dreaming, setting their goals, and applying action to see their dreams come true. For many people in our society today, most dreams consist of financial freedom and the choice to do whatever your heart desires or maybe for better health and fitness levels. The only problem is, nobody knows how they are going to get there.

Think of your dreams as a product. With most products, we sell enable to turn a profit in return. But what happens when you hold on to the product and do nothing? You make no profit off of it whatsoever. You don't obtain the lifestyle you want and you stay in the same situation. Your dreams weren't meant to be locked up within the contents of your mind. You were meant to share your dream with the world. However, it takes a considerable amount of courage to see that your dream doesn't stay in the void of non-existence. Some people who want to achieve

The **ACHIEVER** Effect

their dreams usually try to find ways to make it happen.

This will initiate your mind to open up to any ideas that may help you reach your goals quickly. Beware, this can be dangerous at times, because not every idea is a good one. This could take a considerable amount of thought to figure out. You must know how to separate good ideas from bad ones and how to maximize the potential opportunities presented. So in this chapter, I will be teaching you the means on how you get started on making your dreams a reality. Also, showing how you can weed out bad ideas from good ideas and seize golden or potential opportunities that may help you achieve your dreams.

Getting started on your dream begins with the fundamentals of having an imagination. As discussed in the last chapter, it's no secret that in order to dream, you must use your imagination. By now, you should be sufficient in this area if you performed those exercises mentioned on a daily basis. Now

The **ACHIEVER** Effect

visualize what you want to do and where you want to be in the near future.

It could be your health or your financial setting that you are thinking about. Maybe even both! Now that you have that image in your head, write it down somewhere while the image is still fresh in your mind. Make sure you include when you want to be there by, how much you want to see in your bank account, how you will look, and every single detail about your image. You just created your goals. Now that you have written it down, you can see exactly what you want and when you want it by.

This is very important in goal setting. It's a very great way of keeping track of your progress so you may know exactly where you are on your "achievement bar".

Now I will introduce what I like to call, the "small victory effect". These are mini goals you can complete for you main goal. For example, *let's say that your main goal is to make $500 dollars within the next two weeks. How are you going to achieve this? Now,*

The **ACHIEVER** Effect

let's break that down into tasks you can set that will help you achieve that goal. Such as, mow people's lawn for $20 dollars each. If you were to mow 5 lawns every day, you would have achieved your goal within a week!

Every day that you made $100 dollars was a "small victory". Because then you were even closer to reaching your goal. Most of the wealthy today didn't know how they were going to achieve their dreams when they started. They just knew that they were going to do it. Having an open mind transformed their brains into receivers. Now all sorts of ideas or concepts was entering into their minds and giving them the ammunition needed to "fire" forward and achieve their goals.

Now, I don't have a time frame for when this evolution will happen. It could take days, weeks, or months before you come up with ideas. This depends on how badly you want your dreams to become a reality. One thing is guaranteed; if your "why" is big enough, your "how" will become very clear. To further break this concept down, your "why" is the reason you want to achieve your dreams. It can be any reason you deem fit. It has to be something you are passionate about. Once you figure this out, your "how" will appear. If you don't know much about what you want, do research on it. We live in a time and age where you can find answers to any question you might have at your fingertips. Is your dream worth it?

Believe that your dream will come true and doors will open for you. I once mentioned that not all ideas and opportunities are great ones. Once you decide to go after your dreams and open your mind to receive, a lot of ideas and opportunities will present itself to you. When you are presented with an opportunity, do you often feel a "nudge"? Is your inner self letting you know that you might want to take this path? Most people would describe this as a "gut feeling". However there are two types of this particular feeling. There is a good feeling and a bad feeling. If the idea or concept feels uncomfortable to you, stay away from that.

The **ACHIEVER** Effect

That is God or the universe telling you that this isn't what you need in your life right now. You'll know when the right opportunity will show. You will feel this overwhelming hope fill inside of your heart and soul. You will experience happiness and joy and the image of your dream will be stronger than ever before!

I joined a business called Vemma. I felt something special when I saw the presentation about the business. All I was required to do was to recruit people in to introduce the newest healthy energy drink to the world. At the time I thought, this company is amazing. They provided the world's most complete liquid nutrition to date. And the products tasted amazing! I was absolutely hooked and motivated to recruit everyone I knew into this amazing opportunity. I wanted to share it with the world. A couple of months go by and nobody wanted to join. I learned the hard way that there are a lot of people out there who minds are closed so shut that air couldn't penetrate it! I got angry at the people believe it or not. I would ask myself,

The **ACHIEVER** Effect

why anyone wouldn't want to take advantage of this amazing opportunity.

I heard every excuse you can literally think of. Then one day, I finally decided to watch a documentary one of my coworkers was telling me about called "The Secret". Within the first ten minutes of watching this documentary, I felt my life, my mind changing. I always dreamt of being successful one day and helping people was my biggest dream.

I just didn't know how I was going to do it. But once I fully opened my mind, ideas came and I was forever changed. Even though working alongside this company didn't bare any fruit for me, it led me into writing this book and deciding to speak to people all over to help them find their inner success. Everything happens for a reason. One door was only meant to bring you to another one. Do you see how powerful having a vision or a dream can completely change your life? No matter what your dream may be, it can be reached. And as long as you keep an open mind and believe that you can reach it, life in

The **ACHIEVER** Effect

return will pick the fastest way for you to achieve your dreams and even more.

The **ACHIEVER** Effect

"All men dream: but not equally. Those who dream by night in the dusty recesses of their minds wake in the day to find that it was vanity: but the dreamers of the day are dangerous men, for they may act their dreams with open eyes, to make it possible". – Thomas Edward Lawrence

CHAPTER SEVEN
Unlocking a Closed Mind:

Be Passionate! (Key of Passion)

Passion is the fire behind your drive to accomplish your dreams and goals. It is the very spark that gives you hope and faith that success is right around the corner. Every human being is born with this fire deep within their soul. Throughout history, we've seen that in many cases; where passion played its part to revolutionize the world as we see it today. It gives you the energy you

The **ACHIEVER** Effect

will need to see that your dreams become your reality. This makes passion a great mind opener. Not only does this have the potential to open the doors of your mind, but it swings them wide open! In this chapter, we will rekindle the flame that will drive you right into your success and happiness. You also might discover something new about yourself you would have never known about before.

The essence of passion is very noticeable. You might feel your heart rate skyrocket; your palms getting sweaty, your imagination going to new heights, and your belief becoming stronger than ever! This also depends on what you are passionate about in the first place. Many think of passion in a sexual nature. Although this is the same energy, it can be channeled into many different avenues. Can you imagine if you take that same passion you feel for a man or woman you love and channel it into making your dreams come true? The possibilities would be endless for you. You would be able to achieve anything your heart solely desires. Bodybuilders are a perfect example of what passion can do. Many would disagree and say that it was genetics that made them look that way. But what is genetics if you don't do anything at all to develop? Bodybuilding takes a considerable amount of determination, discipline, and passion to achieve massive results.

Listen to the way they talk about their chosen profession. They speak with emotion as though they cannot live without body building being in their lives. This ladies and gentleman is true passion! What is your passion? What is it that you want to accomplish within your lifetime that you will give up everything for? That feeling you get when you have a good idea of what you really want to do is called passion. This is also the energy that transforms man into geniuses. Every pioneer of change such as inventors, scientists, entrepreneurs, humanitarians, etc. has had some sort of passion for what they did to spur on and make things happen.

Courage also comes along with passion as well. With this tool, getting started or taking

The **ACHIEVER** Effect

that first step is easier. Taking the first step is always the hardest part of starting any dream or goal. Like I discussed in the previous chapter, if your "why" isn't big enough, your "how" won't appear. To further explain this saying, your passion is your "why". I can't stress enough how important passion is to the opening process to opening your mind and clearing any obstacle that may stand in your way. Because once you discover your passion, the answer to achieving your goal will become clearer.

Passion is also a contagious entity on its own. It's been known to move the masses and change anyone's lives it comes near. This comes in handy whenever you might be in a sales position. If the customers you are trying to make a sell to do not see that you are passionate about the product or service you are trying to sell, they will tend to walk out on you. This emotion even helped generals move their armies into action when most soldiers had little to no faith in the cause that they were fighting for.

The **ACHIEVER** Effect

The passion of a leader can give purpose and meaning to his or her followers. So it is absolutely crucial to have this whenever you might find yourself in a leadership position. Let's find out what your passion is. Answer these questions fully and honestly in a "success notepad" of some sort. If you can see what your passion is, you will have a good idea on where your fire burns and zero in on.

"Where is your Passion?"

1. What is it that you REALLY want?

2. What subject can you talk about and get defensive if someone would object to it?

3. What are you ridiculously good at doing?

4. If you could have or do anything, what would it be?

5. What do you love helping people with? How do you most commonly help others?

The **ACHIEVER** Effect

6. What's your favorite section in the bookstore? What's the first magazine you'd pick up at the grocery store?

7. Out of all your current work roles, what would you gladly do for free?

8. What do your friends always tell you you'd be good at, that you should do for a living (i.e. "he'd make a great…)?

9. What are you naturally curious about?

10. What careers do you find yourself dreaming of?

11. What 3-5 dream jobs or businesses can you imagine that would firmly embody your core beliefs about the world?

12. When was the last time you couldn't sleep because you were so excited about what you had to work on? What was it?

13. What would you do if you knew you could not fail?

The **ACHIEVER** Effect

14. When was the last time you were in a state of flow, in the zone and totally lost track of time? What were you doing?

15. Who do you look up to? Who are your mentors? Who inspires you? Why?

16. What do people thank you for?

17. What do you do that makes you feel invincible?

Once you determine where your passion is you can then move on to your action steps. Your "why" by this time should be big enough for a "how" to appear. It's just that easy. My passion is to help people like you and so many others find their purpose or as I like to say, to create their purpose. Life is easy once you get the hang of it and finding your passion will open your mind to new ideas that may help you reach your intended purpose. The more you work toward your passion, the happier and more joyful your life becomes because you are doing what your heart desires. It's time to feel your inner fire burn and shine brightly.

"Every great dream begins with a dreamer. Always remember, you have within you the strength, the patience, and the passion to reach for the stars to change the world." –

Harriet Tubman

The ACHIEVER Effect

CHAPTER EIGHT

Unlocking a Closed Mind:

Being Optimistic (Key of the Optimism)

Being optimistic may very well be the most challenging task to perform in today's world. Optimistic people however can see the bright side to almost every situation or task and can see a way out of anything. Having this skill, in other words, is the same as being hopeful. You may find that having this

The **ACHIEVER** Effect

"skill" will make your life a whole lot easier to handle.

There are ways to bring out the inner optimist in you and open your mind to a lot of concepts about life in general. One thing that causes many people to be less of an optimist is that they only see the negative side of everything instead of the positive. What usually causes this type of mindset may have resulted from the situations and circumstances that may have taken place in their lives. So seeing the positive side may be hard for many to accomplish, but entirely possible. Being optimistic is also a necessary step in order for you to see significant success in your life. Without seeing both sides of a problem or obstacle that may appear in your life, you may find out that achieving your goals may take longer to accomplish.

One way to open your mind and begin the walk on the road of the optimist is to let go of the assumption that the world is against you, or that there is a looming black cloud over your head. It is an assumption that has no

The **ACHIEVER** Effect

basis in reason or science. Sometimes we pick up a flair for pessimism from a parent who made negative assumptions about the world somewhere along the line. Either way, the sooner you can attribute your pessimism to a unique set of circumstances rather than the state of the world itself, the easier it'll be to change your perspective. I understand that you may have gone through or going through situations or circumstances that may not be very favorable. But like we discussed in Chapter 4, it is up to you either the situation or circumstance gets worse or better. Think of how temporary situations are in life. Have you notice that they don't last forever? Just think of how things will be after everything blows over. Have a clear vision of that in your mind and you will get through it faster than you would have if you were to constantly worry.

Another problem that many people have is that they believe that their past will automatically equal their future. Even though things may start off badly doesn't mean it will end badly for you. Things can change as

The **ACHIEVER** Effect

long as your attitude is positive. Life's disappointments are meant to be lessons. Some of us pick up the wrong idea behind the lessons taught. So we tend to allow fear to keep us down.

But as famous motivational speaker *Les Brown* said, "If life knocks you down, try to land on your back. Because if you can look up, you can get up". In other words, keep that optimistic attitude and there is nothing in the world that will be able to keep you down for long. Another thing that will keep you from being optimistic is the thought that you are a victim of your own circumstance. You must see yourself as a cause, not an effect. In order to do this, you must stop thinking about what's happening to you and start thinking about what you can do to make things happen in your favor. If you are not happy with the way that your life is right now, change it. Many people out there really do want to change their life, but allow negative thoughts of what their current circumstances are to stop them from moving forward.

The **ACHIEVER** Effect

This mindset is dangerous to those of you who want to live a successful life. Even though you may be going through or went through times where you tried something new and failed, this is the perfect time to learn of what went wrong and move forward, not to repeat your past mistakes. Now you are able to make better decisions and improve. It goes to what we heard even as children, *"what doesn't kill you makes you stronger"*. Life involves taking many risks every day, and not all of them will end positively. That's what defines risk. But the flip side is that *some* actions will lead to *good* results, and it's generally better to have a mixed bag than to have nothing at all. Ideally, the good stuff will outweigh the bad, but you'll never reach that point unless you put yourself out there and have faith.

To be an optimist, you realize that life is too short to dwell on the small stuff that doesn't matter in the grand scheme of things. Any time spent brooding guarantees nothing but less time to enjoy whatever life might have to offer. I have known people who held

The **ACHIEVER** Effect

themselves back just because they felt as though they weren't "destined" to live a good life. They were born in a low income environment and seen their fair share of struggle growing up. All they ever heard from their parents was how unfair and how impossible life was. So it was hard to be optimistic when everyone around you seems that they lost hope. I truly couldn't blame them for feeling that way.

You will meet challenges along the way. How you meet and react to those challenges will determine if you are ready to receive your success. So look at everything as a two sided coin. There is good and bad to everything. But it would be wise to concentrate on the good and also be aware of the bad. I didn't say concentrate on the bad, just know that its presence is there. To summarize this chapter, let's go over the steps required to obtain optimism.

- Understand that the past does not equal the future

- Remember that life is short

- Let go of the assumption that world and life is against you

- See yourself as a cause, not as an effect

- There are two sides to every situation

Being optimistic opens your mind to the truth behind life. That there is always a good and bad, light and dark, night and day, positive and negative. But to truly be the optimistic type means that you choose to live your life on the positive side of everything. This in turn with yield positives results for you in the future and will cause great success within your life.

"One of the things I learned the hard way was that it doesn't pay to get discouraged. Keeping busy and making optimism a way of life can restore your faith in yourself."-
Lucille Ball

CHAPTER NINE
Unlocking a Closed Mind:

What You Do Have (Key of Gratitude)

It's hard to see what you have already when you see that other people may have more. You see people who may have more money than you, more friends than you, a better car than yours, a bigger house, etc. Some people even look at those who achieved many things as being lucky. They may also believe that they had cheated people to attain their abundance. So you get trapped within this vicious cycle of negative thought.

The **ACHIEVER** Effect

A lot of closed minded people think this way and find it hard to believe that they can attain the same abundance as the rich. But even the wealthy had to start from somewhere. Here is a simple secret that many of the wealthy had used to get to where they are today. It's so simple in fact that you may find it hard to believe that it actually works. The secret is nothing short of gratuity.

When you start to look at your own life and be thankful and grateful for what you already have, you unconsciously allow more room to open up in your life for more blessings. For example, think of everything and everybody you have in your life as of now as junk in your garage. The garage will represent your life. When you concentrate on what you don't have, you tend to forget about everything you do have. So you go out to get more stuff without realizing that you already have a lot. So there is no room for anything extra to enter inside of your garage. Because you didn't take the time to sort everything out, you may have to take back that extra stuff that you just picked up. After you've

The **ACHIEVER** Effect

done that, you tend to be upset because you had to return it. Showing gratitude for what you already have is like sorting and organizing everything within your garage. Wow, you didn't even know you had a floor! Now you have much more space for anything extra that you want.

Another example is the feeling that you feel when someone shows gratitude for what you do for them. When someone does that to you, how do you feel? My guess would be that you would want to do more for that person. Appreciating what you already have also helps you enter into a mindset of absolute clarity. You begin to feel a level of calmness as though you are at peace with yourself and your life. And you start to feel that there is hope for your future. When you mind enters into such a state, it is easier to process positive thoughts. As we know by now, positive thought opens up your mind to receive and understand new ideas. You become a more motivated individual causing you to excel at your job, business, or even schooling. Having a sense of gratitude would

The **ACHIEVER** Effect

also win the respect of those who may be above you in position at your job.

You would be surprised what people would do for you if you show that you are grateful for what they do. If you happen to be in a leadership position or just own your own business with employees, just telling a person how much you appreciate their efforts will not only possibly make their day, but you may also notice that they are performing at a much higher pace than before. To simply put it, *"gratitude is the attitude to have to motivate, inspire, and cultivate people to grow"*. So in return for gratitude, you make more money because your staff is trying to do more for the business.

Being grateful for what you have also helps out in your personal financial field. We can all agree that indebtedness will put you in a negative state of mind. Sometimes you feel as though there is no way out and it's this endless cycle. These times may seem dark, but it's never as bad as it seems. By paying attention to what you have already and moving forward, you find out that the debt will pay for itself.

Did you know that if something were to happen to you where you wouldn't be able to pay them back, whoever you owe will get their money regardless? If you die, your *debts* become part of your estate. Any *assets* would be used to pay off your debts. If you didn't have sufficient assets to cover the debt, the creditor would take a write off. So in the end, what is the sense of worrying about it? With your efforts contributed to showing gratitude for your life, you won't even notice the "troubles" of your life, because they will work themselves in its proper time.

We even have a holiday that solely concentrates on being thankful and grateful. We call this holiday, in the Western world, Thanksgiving. We just have one day out of the year to sit down with close friends and relatives and express our gratitude for everything we experienced so far in the year. Usually during that time, you start to realize there are a lot of things to be grateful for. Just being able to wake up the next day is an

The **ACHIEVER** Effect

accomplishment in itself, and something to be grateful for. Each day is a new day to contribute to your abundant future. When you think of that, does that put you in a better mood? That's the effect that gratuity has on you. When you think about what you do have and begin to be thankful for it, it feels as though you hit the pleasure button in your mind. You begin to enter this mind set of wealth. That is the very feeling you will need to keep in order to solidify your success and see real results.

In order to make things a little easy on you, I will list some gratuity exercises that will help you practice on how to show gratitude. The point behind these exercises is to get you used to having the feeling that follows once you enter a state of gratuity. Let's start off with a morning cup of coffee or breakfast. You can take this time to think about all the things you are grateful for. Sit back and take in everything from how warm the cup of coffee is to the very smell of the coffee itself. Now think about how grateful you are that you have the chance to enjoy the coffee.

The **ACHIEVER** Effect

Thinking about something as small as this would bring you a feeling of joy and appreciation. I would also recommend you go to a park on a beautiful sunny day, sit on a bench, and take in all that you see. Watch the clouds go by and think about how grateful you are to be alive to enjoy it. Another exercise you can do is to think about, if you are working, your job. Not everybody is going to like where they work. You may just be working just to pay the bills and take care of your responsibilities.

So think about how grateful you are to even have the opportunity to work for money. Jobs today are hard to come by and there are a lot of people out of work. This leads back into you going into a positive state of mind. The more grateful you are, the more positivity you will have while you work. Having that mindset will definitely improve your mood at work and you might actually enjoy it!

The last way of getting into the "attitude of gratitude" is to show it to others. Through my personal experience, I have noticed that if you show gratitude toward others, not only

The **ACHIEVER** Effect

do you make other people feel good, but it also gives you a self-gratifying feeling as well. There is nothing quite like the feeling you get when you are making other people smile. For example, show gratitude, if deserving, for people in your work space. One way you can perform this task is to **let your boss know how they're doing a great job** and contributing to the company.

By performing this task, not only are you promoting this person, you are also bringing this person's performance to the spotlight. So now your boss will take even more notice upon them. This in return, will create a better and more positive work area for you. And you might have just made a friend in them as well. A very handy website you can visit is **www.tinybuddha.com** if you want to learn more ways to show your gratitude among other things as well. Gratuity is a very essential tool for your success and one of the most important ways to open your mind. This "technique" will "ready" your mind and spirit to receive all the positive and amazing results that come from showing gratitude.

The **ACHIEVER** Effect

Apply all that you learned in this chapter into your life and watch the magic happen. Life was meant for you to enjoy and share with others. The key of gratitude will open doors for you and present opportunities you would have never dreamed possible!

"You succeed every day of your life when you wake up. Just being able to see another day is an accomplishment on its own. Show gratitude and give thanks". – Lorenzo Sellers

CHAPTER TEN
Unlocking a Closed Mind:
Grow

And Flourish (Key of Love)

There are many different forms of love. Love for a friend is completely different from the love you have for your lover. Love for your lover is completely different from the love you have for what you want to do or what you do for a living. Many people don't live the lives that they really what to live and

The **ACHIEVER** Effect

it's very rare that you would hear from someone that they love what they do. Most of us work just to make ends meet or the meet the expectations set by others. If you don't know if you love what you do, then just ask yourself "do I really love what I do"? If you are not waking up every day for work with a smile on your face and the excitement of a child who's going to the park, chances are you do not love what you do. You do it because it's necessary for your survival.

So it is best that we clarify this before we move on in this chapter. Be truthful with yourself and it will set you and your mind free. Many times people over think the answer to that question. The reason behind that is because if you are surrounded with people who don't go after what they want and accept the way things are given to them, you will believe that is how life is. So you think that you love what you do base off what other people say. They can tell you that you are so "lucky" to have that job or that life is designed to keep you down and only a few will succeed in life and rise to the top.

The **ACHIEVER** Effect

But what they are failing to realize is that there is a simple yet widely unpracticed method to attaining everything that you want. You must love what you do. If you don't, there would be no passion and no desire for you to grow into someone magnificent. Have you ever noticed that people who love what they do tend to be highly efficient in their respectable area? Things work out better for those who love doing their job or career versus those who don't.

And without the love backing your passion, there will be little to no action taken to grow and expand your life. You would be perfectly "content" with where you are. That is often mistaken for love as well. Being content is the same as staying well within your box and looking out the window to the world moving on without you. Nothing is gained through this way of thinking. Although you may not notice it now, but you are slowly losing, piece by piece, a little bit of your soul the longer you wait to leave your "comfort" zone. Because outside of your box, is a world of infinite possibilities and you will never see

The **ACHIEVER** Effect

it if you continue to do something you have no love and passion for.

Love is the final key to opening your mind. This key represents the expansion part of your opening process. Without room to grow within your mind, your life cannot grow. Your thoughts control what happens to you within your life and how you live it. Think of it this way; your mind is just like the game called "The Sims". You start off by how much land you have to build on. If you only have four squares of land, you won't have much to work with. You won't be able to have much and your world is very limited. This is how the mind of a closed minded person looks. Throughout this book, we were slowly learning how to expand a closed mind to build more within its world. This started off with positivity. You are looking at your four squared world and not getting depressed about it. Then we moved into your imagination. You can see where your four squared world expands and grows. It's massive and you can do anything within it.

The **ACHIEVER** Effect

Now your dream kicks in. This is where you are going to place your passion. Your dream is to now create or attain more land to build on. You used your imagination and transformed that into your dream for a massive world of endless possibly and joy. This is when you make your dream into your passion. You are now obsessed with creating this world! This will ensure that your new world becomes a reality. Then you start on the maintenance of this world by being an optimist. Being able to be open to any idea that may contribute to your world is essential. You can build more houses or amusement parks on your land. Maybe you can throw a couple of recreational parks in there. The idea behind this is that your world would be more "well rounded".

Then we move onto gratitude. This alone will create more quality to your world. Instead of allowing the thoughts of "I wish I had more stuff to put on there", you are grateful that you have the materials you require. This will give you more of a sense of fun added to this project. You have all that

The **ACHIEVER** Effect

you need to build your perfect world. Here we are back to the final ingredient of your project. Love contributes to this in a very huge way. You now have the patience to continue with your expansion. At this point, it doesn't matter to you how long it will take to get there. I call this the "reaching effect". You will keep reaching for your goal. You won't even notice the time you spent or how much you have already built. By the time you look back on your world, you will see an even more massive world that you dreamt about in the beginning.

You expanded well beyond what you originally planned. And now you will be able to reap the benefits of it. This also applies to what you do in your life as well. Anything that you set out to do in your life at this point, make sure that you love what you do. Without it, you will have a hard time staying committed and your dreams will never be fulfilled. It also must be something you can do 7 days a week and smile each day that you do it. One definite way of telling if you love what you do is if you can answer this question truthfully. *Would you do it for free?* Although a simple question, you will find out that many people can't answer that question being at their current jobs. Granted, there are some people out there who love their jobs and would be more than happy to work all the time.

Society has named those who love to work around the clock. They call those types of people "workaholics". However, I can guarantee that they wouldn't want to work so hard for no pay. *So why not be a workaholic for something you love to do?* It is human nature to want to live life freely. It's very seldom that you will meet anyone who wants to live life under someone else's rules and time. Time is our most precious commodity; because that is the one thing you cannot buy back. So why not live life the way you want to while you still have the time to accomplish it?

Once you found that one thing that you love to do, go after it! Don't waste any more time living within a box. The world is literally waiting for you to come out and

The **ACHIEVER** Effect

show it exactly who you are and what you bring to the table. It's about time you do what makes you happy and there are a lot of ideas and concepts out there that will take you down the most efficient and harmonious way to accomplishing your dreams and goals. Follow everything you have learned in these previous chapters and you will live with the benefits of having an open mind.

"Don't aim for success if you want it: just do what you love and believe in it and it will come naturally"- David Frost

Chapter Eleven

Surpassing Your Limitations:

Road to Riches and Wealth

We place certain limitations on ourselves in response to what we perceive as possible. As children, we didn't have a limit on what we thought was possible. In short, our limitations are literally set by others as well as our environment as we grow into adulthood. It's no secret that children absorb information at a faster rate than your average adult. So whatever is said or implemented

The **ACHIEVER** Effect

around our children will be "inherited" into their thought process and will affect how they react to situations or what they accomplish within their lives. These limitations bearing down in our minds are simply illusions that were set by past events.

But how do we break down these "barriers" and surpass our current limitations? The answer is simple. Live your life by the day and live it as though it's your last. It is known that whenever you are faced with a life or death situation, your mind is working overtime to figure out ways to escape the set situation. So you find yourself doing things you never thought you could do before. Your senses physically and mentally are heightened to levels you may have not experienced before. In sports, boxers use this technique. In many cases, boxers use their fear of being hurt to their advantage.

Their agility, speed, and power are increased to deal with their current situation. You may use this same method when it comes to any life situation that may come along. Think of the mouse cornered by the

The **ACHIEVER** Effect

cat. The mouse is now at its most dangerous state of mind and it's most creative. Now apply a human mind to this equation. When one faces poverty right in the face, you would be surprised how resourceful and creative he or she can be. Any limitation that you thought you had will go flying right out the window and now your mind is completely open to any idea or concept that will help you escape that situation. You basically devote all your energy every day to accomplish your goals as though you will not see tomorrow.

Most millionaires today faced poverty before they reached the height of their riches and wealth. It was during that time that they became creative and brought into existence ideas, concepts, and inventions that helped them accumulate their mass riches. They figured out a secret that most people today are still searching for. The reality of this is that the answer is so obvious and so simple that people can't grasp the fact that it works. Living your life to the fullest each day will help you accumulate an abundance of wealth, happiness, and joy. Your limitations would be a thing of the past and nothing will be out of your reach.

Another way of surpassing your limitations is practice. Surely you heard quote "practice makes perfect". Well I'm here to tell you that it's not true. Practice will only make improvement because there is nothing "perfect" in this world. The term "perfect" means that there is no need for further improvement. This means that there would be no further growth and you set a limit for yourself. So who wants to be perfect? It's a capping statement to your hidden potential. Potential is a never ending power you have to accomplish anything. We all have this latent power inside of us and the only thing that is holding most of our potential back is the limitations that we set for ourselves.

If you believe that you have a limit, then one will be set for you. Just as we discussed in the first chapter, your thoughts have unimaginable power and control over what happens in your life. Simply believe that you have no limit to what you can accomplish and it will become your reality. We all carry

The **ACHIEVER** Effect

a universe around ourselves and what we think and do effects that universe. Any thoughts of you not accomplishing anything noteworthy in your life will become a reality. So you really do hold yourself back from greatness even though our thoughts come from things we witnessed or experienced for ourselves. This is when you must develop a sense of decisiveness. Being indecisive will only prolong your greatness from seeing the surface. So you must be clear on exactly what you want despite what you may experience in life.

You should not allow situations and circumstances detour you away from what you set out to do. If everybody allowed their "limitations" to stand in their way, we would still be living back in the caveman days. Even in the caveman era, one created the wheel. It can be assumed that the caveman who accomplished this feat didn't allow his lack of "education" limit him. All he had was his imagination and his will to create. Sometimes that is all you really need to become successful. The key here is to know your self-worth. Knowing what your worth is will create that reality for you. If you believe that you are worth 1 million dollars, then that, with action, will become the actual reality that you live. In order to attain more, you must become more. You must immerse yourself into a mindset of absolute certainty. You become what you consistently think about. So if you are always thinking about how poor you may be, then that is the lifestyle you will live until you change your outlook.

Your thoughts effect your actions, giving you exactly the results that come with the thought you had. If you want to be a motivational speaker, you will find yourself listening to more speakers every day trying to adopt their ways and techniques. We live in a world today where information can be gathered at the comfort of our own homes. Knowledge is power. The more you know about what you want to do, the easier it will be to accomplish. But having riches isn't the dream of every individual out there. Some people actually just want to live life their way and there is nothing wrong with that. However, know that every decision you make has its benefits and/or downfalls. For example, you hear that you can say certain stuff to your boss. In many cases, and I know some of you experienced this as well, you can't stand up for yourself to your boss without there being some type of rebuttal. Well, I'm here to tell you that you can say anything you want to your boss. But if they don't like what you have to say, it could be your last day there.

But if you were truly wronged for standing up for yourself and others because you and they were treated badly, then you weren't meant to be there. This may not always be the case. Maybe you might have had a different approach other than your employer to help the business. But remember that people fear change, so they might over react and think you are trying to steal their job instead of helping them progress. This is called thinking as an individual, which is one of the traits of the wealthy and a clear sign that you weren't mean to work for somebody

The **ACHIEVER** Effect

else. In the military, we call this the leadership trait.

Millionaires and leaders think very differently from everyone else. Not just about money, about everything. The time and energy everybody else spends attempting to conform, both parties spend creating their own path. Since thoughts impact actions, people who want to be wealthy should think in a way that will get them to that goal. Independent thinking doesn't mean doing the opposite of what the rest of the world is doing; it means having the courage to break down your personal barriers and follow what is important to you. So, the lesson here is to forge your own way, and let your success drive you to financial spoils rather than doing it the other way around and trying to chase the money. For what you chase will always be allusive to you.

But thinking as an individual is only a fraction of what it means to be a leader and/or millionaire. Based off of the research I conducted talking to various millionaires and successful business owners here in San

The **ACHIEVER** Effect

Diego, they have concluded that enable for a person to climb the ladder to wealth, you must have a vision. The vision is a means to meet your end. Millionaires are creative visionaries with a positive attitude. In other words, wealthy people not only have big dreams, they also *believe* they will come true. As such, wealth seekers should set lofty goals and not be afraid of uncharted territories. The uncharted territory holds most of the money to be made and has endless possibilities of untold riches. So dare to be different and embrace your vision!

Now let's say that you may have a certain set of skills that can help you achieve your vision. But there are areas that are in need improvement before you can move forward. At this point, you could try to improve all areas to ensure your success or you can create a "Mastermind" group. Millionaires usually hone in and develop the skills that they are good at. The best way to supplement the skills that they lack falls into the help of their mastermind group. Millionaires tend to partner with others to supplement their

The **ACHIEVER** Effect

weaker skills. If you don't know what you are good at, poll friends and family. Use training and mentors to refine and develop your strong skills.

A lot of people dislike going into a salesman position. The idea of going door to door usually crosses the minds of many who hear the word salesman. Salesmanship is more than that. Millionaires are consistently presenting their ideas and persuading others to buy into them. Great salesmen are oblivious to critics and naysayers. In other words, they don't take "no" for an answer. Millionaires also have amazing social skills. In fact, social skills are more important than IQ when it comes to making millions. Just look at Donald Trump. His fortune has fluctuated over the years, but his ability to sell himself has always brought him back among the ranks of celebrity millionaires.

There is a quiet secret that a lot of people would like to know. How do you make a lot of money? Well, the answer may shock many people at how simple it is. Making millions happens when people take money from their pockets and give it to you in exchange for a product or service. So being social is probably the only way you are going to create a large amount of income. *Is this simplistic by nature? Yes. Is it hard to do? Not if you are willing to open your mind to different ideas and concepts.*

Have you ever heard the saying, "it takes money to make money"? Even though that may be true, it's not always the case. To invest into something that you want can be an array of ways. But let's further discuss what it means to invest into something. There are three different types of investing. The three types are *money*, *time*, and *energy*. There are many opportunities out there that will require an initial investment. This frightens a lot of people because of the fear of not getting a return on that investment and one of the primary reasons why there are so few business owners out there today. With money, it takes a considerable amount of courage to get over that fear to invest. A little money now can make you millions in the future. Now that is something to think about.

The **ACHIEVER** Effect

Your time can also be an investment on its own. If you simply would invest a lot of your time now into building your empire, less of your time will be needed in the future when your empire is up and running on its own. When I was in the MLM (multi-level marketing) business, I heard every excuse why someone couldn't invest the time or money to ensure that they have a better financial future. The problem with most people is that they can't believe in something they can't see as of yet. To them it's all about the here and now. Investing is a foreign word to them and can be considered as a bad thing. Even if they had a dream, they just won't go after it because it might pose a risk. In other words, they are simply not risk takers. "The bigger the risk, the bigger the payoff". If you invest little, then that is exactly what you will get back.

Investing your energy has helped the top money makers of the world make their millions. The more energy you put into something, the more you will get out of it. Very rarely has anyone who didn't invest anything into their goals got anything back from it. We live in a world of equal exchange. If you don't move, then how can you expect for anything to change?

As we discussed in previous chapters, passion is the driving force behind your action. If the passion isn't there, nine times out of ten, there will be no action involved and taking the risk would be out of the question. Passion sees past the risk that is necessary for your success. Athletes, leaders, entrepreneurs, and any other profession all use a high level of drive and conviction to ensure their success. Enjoying your work allows you to have the discipline to work hard at it every day. People who interact with money for a living, bankers for example, often love creating new deals and persuading others to complete a transaction. But finding your dream job may take time. The average millionaire doesn't find it until age 45, and tends to be 50 before becoming a millionaire. The purpose of this book is to help you, especially the young, open your mind and figure out what your dream may be and to act

The **ACHIEVER** Effect

on it before you reach that age or even if you are already there, to serve as a catalyst.

Every day, there is somebody out there setting a limit on what they can really do. You must extinguish those negative thoughts about yourself and see the light that is your future. There is nothing embarrassing about going after your dream and you shouldn't allow other people to tell you otherwise. Surpassing your limitations and realizing that it never existed is a choice that only you can make.

There are three different types of people in the world. There are people who won't allow "limitations" to stop them and make things happen, there are people who allow "limitations" to stop them and sit in the crowd and watch things happen and then there are people who always ask the question, *"Whoa! What just happened?"* At this point you must ask yourself a serious question. *Which one are you?*

The **ACHIEVER** Effect

Thoughts:_____
_____
_____
_____
_____
_____

"If you limit your choices only to what seems possible or reasonable, you disconnect yourself from what you truly want, and all that is left is compromise."- Robert Fritz

CHAPTER TWELVE

The Secret to a Joyful and Abundant Life

It's no secret that you probably want to live your life by your terms. For a lot of people, this means that you must have an abundance of money to do so. By chance, *was that your exact thought?* To live life by your terms would mean that you must change your mind set. Remember this from the first chapter, in order to change your universe, it must begin within yourself. You are the centerpiece to your own universe and your

The **ACHIEVER** Effect

life. The best way to describe this *theory* is to relate to one having a dream.

If you are self-aware while you are dreaming, you can control how your dream goes and work it to your advantage with a single thought. Granted, life is nothing like a dream. You won't see crazy things popping up out of nowhere in reality. However, your thoughts do control your actions therefore controlling the outcome of your life. In a dream, anything you think about just pops up as soon as you can conceive it. There is no lag time between your thoughts and the materialization of your thoughts. But in reality, there is a lag time. This is in good taste because the last thing you want is your thoughts materializing as soon as you think it. We were all born with a power to create anything we want with our thoughts. You are connected to a power that directs current events, creates something from nothing, and controls what you experience in this life. Isn't it a wonderful concept to live by? Many of your richest and most powerful people understood this concept and applied it to their own lives pushing them to unforeseen levels of prosperity.

I was raised to believe in God and to put faith unto Him. A quote I heard my entire life was, "through Him, all things are possible". I still believe in that even in today's world. I even found that there are similarities between the power of our thoughts and the teachings of religions. When it all comes down to it, in order to live a prosperous life, we must have faith in our own abilities, act on it, and in my religion, God will see it through. By no means am I forcing my religion on you. The basic idea behind this is that there is a great power that enables us to create our own purpose. So it would help to know exactly how to control this "power" and create the life that you always wanted to live.

We live in a world where there are negative energies everywhere you go. But just because the energies are there doesn't mean you have to let it influence your life. Crime, gangs, fights, wars, and overall hate are all contributing factors to those negative energies I was referring to. There are many of us who were born into that reality and couldn't see the light at the end of the tunnel or believed that there is no light to begin with. I used to live on a street such as this where you would hear gun shots and police cars speeding by almost every night. Even though I was a child and couldn't comprehend fully what was going on at the time, I slowly but surely learned as I got older. I know what it is like to have little to no hope of ever getting ahead in life. But after realizing that my life is controlled by how I see it, magnitudes of changes had occurred. It's time to tell you exactly how to create positive changes in your life and to live abundantly.

There are two types of mindsets that we as human beings adapt to. There is the *scarcity mindset* and the *abundance consciousness*. We'll start off with the scarcity mindset first. Most people live with this type of mindset. It explains a great deal why most people still live the lives they don't desire. This does nothing but rob you from living your life and making your own rules. I'm not saying you

The **ACHIEVER** Effect

are going to break laws. I mean to live your life fully with joy and happiness being a part of it. A person who lives their life with this mindset tends to:

Criticize……..

Hold a grudge……..

Blame others for their failures…..

Say they keep a journal but really don't…….

Think they know it all…….

Operate from a transactional perspective……

Secretly hope others fail………

Don't know what they want to be…….

Never set goals……..

Exude anger………

Horde information and data…….

Talk about people……..

Fly by their seat of their pants……

The **ACHIEVER** Effect

Fear change………

Watch TV everyday……….

Take all the credit of their victories…….

And have a sense of entitlement……

You tend to find this way of thinking within the workplace, your friends and family, and everywhere you go. I know many of you have seen someone exude at least one of these traits, if not all. Have you ever caught yourself having at least one of these traits? Now that you look back on that, how does that make you feel? I know that I had a lot of these traits at one point in my life. Living with this mindset is poisonous, and you are unconsciously holding yourself back from living a great life. For those of you wanting to know how this affects your income, it completely blocks you from attaining wealth. There are people out there with this mindset and still are rich. But the question arises, are they happy? Having money is one thing, but having money and living your life happily is another.

The **ACHIEVER** Effect

That is what true wealth is. You are happy and stable in all areas of your life. Living abundantly doesn't take much effort at all. It takes more energy being negative (scarcity mindset) than it does being positive (abundance consciousness). Living and thinking abundantly will bring you abundance. Just like we discussed before, what you put out will come back like a boomerang. You become what you think you are. Those who have an abundance consciousness tend to:

Compliment………

Forgive others……….

Accept responsibility for their failures………..

Keep a journal……..

Want others to succeed……

Keep a "to-be" list………

Set goals and develop life plans……….

Continuously learn……………

The **ACHIEVER** Effect

Operate from a transformational perspective……..

Keep a "to-do/project" list……….

Embrace change………..

Exude joy………..

Share information and data…………

Talk about ideas………..

Read every day……………

Give other people credit for their victories…….

And have a sense of gratitude…….

Most people believe that the reason a lot of wealthy people are happy is because of the size of their bank account. The size of their bank account is only of fraction of the reason, but not the main reason. It's true that the money gives them options on what they want to do. But like I stated, it's only a fraction. They are abundant in all areas of their life. This means that they may have people who care about them, people who love them, accomplishing that dream that they had, going to all the vacation spots they dreamt of going to, earned the respect of others, may have helped countless people within their lifetime, have loyal friends that had been there for them since the beginning, etc.

You will find out that the people who follow this abundance check list are living the lives that they want to live. They are connected and in tune with their inner self and spirit. They did what they wanted to do instead of doing what others wanted them to do. In other words, they had set their own standard on life instead of accepting the standard of others. The truth is that you will come across people who will attempt to bring you back to the scarcity mindset and you will know who they are. But only let this be an attempt, not a succession. By practicing these traits and habits, you will find yourself being a lot happier and cheerful. You will experience things that other people with a negative mindset won't ever have the chance to.

The **ACHIEVER** Effect

If having a wealthy lifestyle is your goal, open your mind to this concept and allow it to take you to where you want to be because nothing else will. Feed that fire that is within your heart and soul and go out there and achieve your dream. It doesn't matter where you are from or what happened to you in your past. If you can still walk, talk, move, and live, then you can achieve. You have more power within you than anyone could even fathom and the only one who can bring it out is you. Situation and circumstances will always come up in your life. How you handle those events is completely up to you. Success only comes to those who desire it and work toward it. Having the right attitude and mindset is crucial for this journey to your success.

Many allow bad circumstances and situations get the better of them. The trick to getting past those times is to smile. Smiling will indeed brighten up your mood and open your mind to how you can move past the hard times. This is also the way to live abundantly. You attract what you are. I'm sure you heard

The **ACHIEVER** Effect

the quote, let's call a spade a spade. If it walks like a duck, acts like a duck, and quacks like a duck, it's not a bear. Chances are great that it's a duck. This means that if you were to walk the part, talk the part, and act the part, you are the part that you want to play. *What is it that you want to become? What type of lifestyle you wish to live?* When it is all said and done, it is still your life. The secret to living a joyful and abundant life is to give often, love deeply, laugh often, and go for your dreams because no one else will make your dreams a reality but you.

"Take a step in faith. You don't have to see the whole staircase, just take the first step"- Martin Luther King Jr.

PART II: Walking the Path

CHAPTER THIRTEEN

What It Means To Discover Your Dream

Discovering your dream may come to you in many forms. It may come to you in a dream, when you are meditating, while you are working on your job, while talking to friends or family, or you might have discovered it when you were a child. Whenever and however you may find it, one

The **ACHIEVER** Effect

thing will always remain the same. You will feel a sense of joy when you realize what it is. Usually your dream will be something that you will enjoy doing. Ask yourself, *will I do this for free?* This is a great way to indicate what your dream job or profession may be.

By doing what you love to do, not only are you in tune with your passion, but you are also extending your own life force! It has been proven that when you are doing what you want to do in your life, your stress is lowered and your health is increased, therefore expanding your life. Far too many people are stressing themselves out over a job that they don't even like. By not acting on your dream and doing what you love to do, you are literally killing yourself spiritually bit by bit every single day! Depression seems to be a normal condition for you, and stress has made a home within your life. This in turn could drive everything that you love away from you. Who in the world would want that? Chasing after your dream would be a benefit for you and anyone else you are around.

The **ACHIEVER** Effect

You will notice that your mood has picked up, you have a lot more energy to do more activities, and your love life would skyrocket! The benefits also include:

- More confidence
- Feel a lot younger
- Illness becomes scarce
- Less stress

The list goes on, but believe me, it is all positive changes that you will experience for yourself. The reason why many people are not doing what they love is because of the fear of not being able to take care of themselves or their family financially. This fear is understandable. However, there is a "myth" about following your bliss or your dream. "Do what you love to do and the money will follow".

To my experience in this area, I would have to say that this "myth" is indeed a fact. When you are doing what you love, the money becomes completely irrelevant. This goes back into that question about doing it for free. You will find people out there who will say that this isn't true. But before you take their advice, check out their situation first. Are they truly happy with where they are in their life? Are they making the money they would like to make? Are they always stressed and complaining about how hard life is?

It is also said that if you do what you love, you will never "work" a day in your life. With any job or business, you often need to do things you wouldn't choose to do. For me, I love to write and motivate people. So my dream is to become a world renowned author, life coach, and motivational speaker for achieving personal success. My weakest skill however is marketing. So when I try to market myself, it seems like work to me. This doesn't mean I don't market myself. I hire other people who love to market and promote people to help me in this area. It's all about freedom of choice. Are you moving toward making your dream a reality or someone else's dream? When you are doing things to make your dream come true, it won't seem like work. Have you ever caught yourself watching the clock consistently throughout your work day? At that point, you can't wait till its quitting time. This is a clear indication that you are "working".

When you are chasing your dream, it will seem like there isn't enough time in the day! It's all about the perception. When you discover your dream and decide to act on it, you must go in knowing that even though you are about to do what you love to do, there are going to be some parts of the deal that will seem less exciting to you than the parts that you love to do. This is what it means to do what you love for work. In a psychological experiment that took place in 1956, it showed people are more likely to find intrinsic motivation when they're paid very little to do a task. When the monetary compensation increases, suddenly the money becomes the motivation, and as a result, it feels less enjoyable. I personally talked to people who are massively successful in their

The **ACHIEVER** Effect

business, but have no passion for it. So when discovering your dream, make sure that it is something that you can see yourself doing for years to come.

It takes great courage to act on your dream and it involves stepping out of your "comfort zone". We will go further into that later on in this book. I'm not suggesting you drop everything you got going on now to chase your dream. The reality of it is that not everybody is in a position to do that. However, it is entirely possible to start on your dream at any point in your life. But one must be wise about doing so. There are certain needs that need to be met before you start your journey. In 1940-50s, Abraham Maslow created the Hierarchy of Needs model. This theory still remains valid even in today's world for understanding human motivation, management training, and personal development. This is key information to key when deciding you want to go after your dreams. Without even knowing it, we ensure that these needs are met before we start any venture. For some

The **ACHIEVER** Effect

people, some of these needs were not being met at all, but they still did what they love to do and became massively successful. So this theory may not reign true for some people, but most.

The first and most basic level of needs that need to be met are your biological and physiological needs. They are your basic life needs such as *air, food, water, shelter, sex, homeostasis, excretion, and sleep.* The second level above that would be your safety needs such as *security of body, employment, resources, morality, family, health, and of property*. The third level above safety needs would be your love and/or belonging needs such as *family, friendship, and sexual intimacy.* Above that on the fourth level of needs would be esteem such as *self-esteem, confidence, achievement, respect for others, and respect by others.* The need of self-actualization would be the top of this pyramid. This involves *morality, creativity, spontaneity, problem solving, lack of prejudice, and the acceptance of facts.*

The **ACHIEVER** Effect

It's all about knowing exactly where you stand in life. This may seem like a lot to know, but in actuality, it is a pretty simple concept to grasp. For most people who discover what their dream may be, you feel as though you have a purpose in life. Whether it means you are helping people physically, mentally, or spiritually, you feel as though you were meant to accomplish this goal. The grand "unanswered" question to life is "what is the purpose to my existence?" My answer to you would be that your purpose is what you create for yourself. There is no predestined answer for you. God created everyone with the gift of free will. If you will it so, it will come to pass. So whatever you believe your purpose to be, then that will be your destiny. You literally set your own rules. I have a saying I like to live by; your situation today is based off of the decision you made yesterday.

Here is a basic formula you can use when it comes to the process of your dream shifting into your reality:

- ✓ YOUR THOUGHT becomes

The **ACHIEVER** Effect

- ✓ YOUR VISION which turns into
- ✓ YOUR DREAM then creates
- ✓ YOUR PASSION which moves you
- ✓ INTO ACTION

Once you act on your dream, you are actively bringing your dream into the physical world. Then you will be living your dream as it is now your reality. This is pretty simple right? Because this is such a simple formula, many people don't adhere to it. You will always hear people say that it's too simple to work. This process has worked for many of our successful people today. Just by shifting your thoughts from the "can't" position to the "can" position, you are now creating an opportunity for yourself to move forward and achieve whatever you set out to do.

This is what it means to discover your dream. You will find your reason to live. If you had a dream from way back, dust it off and find a way to act on it. If you are just now discovering what your dream actually is,

The **ACHIEVER** Effect

gauge your life and see what you can do to move forward to it. Achieving your dream is closer than you realize. Discovering what that dream may be is the first step to you living the life you always wanted. *What is your dream?* It's time to move into action and take those steps down the path of the dream chaser. They don't have to be big steps. Any movement forward is a positive change to your life and one step closer to you achieving your goal.

CHAPTER FOURTEEN

Who You Are

What defines you as a person? Is it the friends you keep? What about your personal history or your past? None of these things will tell you where you are in life and it definitely won't define who you are. Only you are capable of doing that task. This is where you have the advantage! As children, we all heard our parents and teachers tell us at one point in our young lives that we can be anything we want to be. This was indeed solid and valuable advice. You are who you

The **ACHIEVER** Effect

believe yourself to be. Your thoughts control the aura or persona that you carry.

This in turn will move things around for you to manifest your thoughts into actuality. You are the creator of your current reality. What happens to you is all determined by the mindset that you carry. For example, if you believe that you are a professional speaker, then you will find yourself thinking like one. This goes for any profession out there that you may want to endeavor. This is when that formula I mentioned back in the first chapter comes to play. In order for your thoughts to take over your actions, you must envision yourself as a professional speaker. If you feel satisfaction from that vision, you will find out that the thought of being one will consume you. This is when you will find out that your dream, if you didn't already know it, is to be a professional speaker. This will fire up the passion within you to attain the title of speaker.

And then out of nowhere, you will find yourself acting like one. Your actions will then be controlled by the passion of being a professional speaker. You will start walking, acting, and speaking like you are already at the pinnacle of your chosen profession. Now a lot of people would say that's called being fake. But in the most humble opinion, it is called being real. In order to become something that you want to be, you must learn the art of imitation. This is the most basic form of learning and it is still a very effective method.

But just like Superman who has the dreaded kryptonite as his weakness, we all have some weak spots that could weaken our resolve or completely kill any kind of hope we have to do better. One thing that could possibly kill your resolve before you even get started is the crowd or friends you choose to associate yourself with. That saying, "birds of a feather flock together" reigns true in many cases. The type of crowd you hang with will determine how far you go in life. If you, for example, chose to follow negative people, then the chances are high that you, yourself will wind up just as negative as they are. This could be a damaging road block for you and

The **ACHIEVER** Effect

none to take lightly. We all value the opinions that our friends may have. Whether it is on the career path you are on to the choices you make on chasing your dream. If you are surrounded by friends who complain about how unfair life is, then it will be hard for you to see life in any other way because you value their input.

In order to see what type of friends you have, you need to think about the type of effect that they have on your life. Ask yourself, *are they encouraging me daily to go after my dreams and live a happy life or are they consistently coming up with excuses why I shouldn't strive for more?* A great rule of thumb would be if they are not an encouraging bunch, it is best you cut ties with them. This may seem cold at first, but it is vital that you allow no one to hold you back from living the life that you want to live. Surround yourself with people who want the same things you want. These are people who want to be more than what they are right now and who is always wanting to learn more. In other words, you need to be around people

The **ACHIEVER** Effect

with open minds. To my experience in this area, I surrounded myself with people who are no stranger to a little bit of hard work. You want your circle of friends to be an external version of you. What this means is that you are who you surround yourself with. So if you are a negative and miserable person, then that is the type of people you will attract and eventually be surrounded by. However, if you are a positive and uplifting person, then that is what you will attract into your inner circle.

Another potential road block for you is your family. I know that statement definitely raised a few eyebrows. Here you will find people who may tell you that they know exactly who you are. Even though they would like to think they know who you are, only you would know that information. No one knows who you are until you discover that for yourself. In some cases, family members may be the main ones to bring you down off your "high horse". A lot of people believe that anyone who wants to see themselves as more is arrogant or conceited.

The **ACHIEVER** Effect

So they will do their best to bring you down. And this action isn't spurred on by hate, but by love. They just don't want to see you get hurt or experience "failure". Even though their intentions may be good, the effect is still the same. This may stop you just because you may feel as though they disapprove of your new decision. Hearing the word "no" from your family members could hurt. But that doesn't mean that you have to accept it.

You may hear things like, *"this isn't like you"* or *"you aren't capable of doing this or that"*. And we can't forget my all-time favorite line, *"that has never been done before. What makes you think you can do it?"* You shouldn't allow these words to phase you. Only you would know what you are capable of. Think about this one for a few moments. We all have a special something within us. During the creation period of human life, there are millions of sperm that makes its way to the egg. But only one will achieve human life. You were that one sperm who beat all the competition and achieved life. So you cannot say that there isn't something special about you. You have literally been achieving greatness before you were even born!

Simply find out what makes you unique from everybody else. We were all blessed with our own unique way of thinking. And if you are on the path to achieving your dream, you need to figure that out. It could be your ideas or your unique concepts that could change the way everything works! There is a power deep within us all that can change the flow of our lives. In some cases, there are people out in the world today whose power can help empower other people. Sometimes, we learn who we are after we already have taken that first step toward making our dreams into a reality through the experiences we go through while on the journey.

The next question you must ask yourself is, *"what inspires me?"* This is the key to your inner passion and the reason why you even started the journey in the first place. What is the purpose behind your actions? I would suggest that you write all these answers down in a notepad. Along the long path to your

The **ACHIEVER** Effect

infinite greatness, you will arrive at points where you might forget why you even started the journey. By writing it down and keeping it with you, it can remind you of the purpose of your journey and spur you to keep moving. It's a great motivation tactic that has been used for centuries. Even though a notepad wasn't always used, there was something that one might possess that symbolizes one's inspiration or your reason for being.

Inspiration has taken many people of history to heights of untold riches and wealth such as Thomas Edison, Andrew Carnegie, Leonardo Da Vinci, Bill Gates, Oprah Winfrey, etc. Anyone you can think of that has had massive success in their lives had some sort of inspiration that sparked their fire to accomplish their dreams. Once you achieve self-awareness, finding your dream and accomplishing it is all too easy of a task.

CHAPTER FIFTEEN

Comfort Zone

I feel as though in order for you to be ready to step out of your "comfort zone", you must first know what it is. The comfort zone is the one reason why so many people fail to even begin their journey to untold riches and wealth. This zone would be considered at a "limiter" and should be disposed of immediately. It is important and quite crucial to your success to learn how to avoid being trapped in the comfort zone. One of the main reasons why most of the successful people in the world achieved extraordinary success is because they were able to think differently, take risks and move out of their comfort zones. Most people remain unsuccessful and stay in their comfort zones because of fears, limiting beliefs, habits or simply because of laziness. In fact, our comfort zone is a place in which we feel safe and secure and where there is no sense of risk. It is made up of the known, the accepted and the expected and it can be physical, emotional, intellectual or financial.

The comfort zone is a behavioral state within which a person operates in an anxiety-neutral condition, using a limited set of behaviors to deliver a steady level of performance, usually without a sense of risk. A person's personality can be described by his or her comfort zones. Highly successful persons may routinely step outside their comfort zones, to accomplish what they wish. A comfort zone is a type of mental conditioning that causes a person to create and operate mental boundaries. Such boundaries create an unfounded sense of security. Like inertia, a person who has

The **ACHIEVER** Effect

established a comfort zone in a particular axis of his or her life, will tend to stay within that zone without stepping outside of it. To step outside their comfort zone, a person must experiment with new and different behaviors, and then experience the new and different responses that occur within their environment.

This refers to any endeavor that you may want to partake in such as acting on your dream. I'm not saying once you step outside of your "box" you won't ever see it again. That would be a false statement and the whole point to this chapter is to educate you on the ups and downs of stepping out. The truth is that you may wind up back in a comfort zone as you move forward and upward. There isn't a single achiever out there who would say that you don't ever get into a comfortable state again. You must always challenge yourself to avoid getting into another comfort zone.

For most people, moving out of the comfort zone can be very frightening and embarrassing. But it is certainly the single

The **ACHIEVER** Effect

most important step we can make towards achieving peak performance in anything we do. We must take actions we have not previously taken if we expect to achieve different results than what we have been getting. Tony Robbins once said "If you do what you've always done, you'll get what you've always gotten."

One of the best ways to move out of our comfort zone is to face our fears and do the things we fear most. In fact, most of our fears are unnecessary and counterproductive. We frighten ourselves unnecessarily about things that will never happen. Franklin D Roosevelt was right when he said "The only thing we have to fear is fear itself." We should face our fears and see them for what they really are. Once we face our fears, the death of fear is certain. What are fears anyway? According to psychologists, F.E.A.R is just "False Evidence Appearing Real". We should make it a habit to do something that frightens us every day. The more we push ourselves out of our comfort zone and do the things that scare us, the easier it becomes.

The **ACHIEVER** Effect

We can also get out of our comfort zone and achieve success by breaking our habits. Our habits determine our outcomes and our negative habits always create negative consequences that prevent us from getting the success we want. In order to become more successful, we can start by replacing our bad habits with more productive ones. Research shows that it takes only 21 days to develop a habit. According to Paul Getty, the individual who wants to reach the top in business must appreciate the might and force of habit. He must be quick to break those habits that can break him and hasten to adopt those practices that will become the habits that help him achieve the success he desires.

Another great way to get out of our comfort zone is to get rid of our self-limiting beliefs. These limiting beliefs are things we believe about ourselves that place limits on our aptitudes. Examples of self-limiting beliefs are when we think that we are not good enough to do certain things or we are not intelligent enough to succeed in life. Most of these beliefs are not true, but they make us stay in our comfort zones and play small in life. We can eliminate our limiting beliefs by becoming aware of them, identifying them and replacing them with more positive beliefs.

In order to succeed in anything, we have to break free of our comfort zone, and step into the unknown. Getting out of our comfort zone is not always easy and often requires lots of hard work, discipline and persistence. Brian Tracy once said, "Ninety to ninety-five percent of people will withdraw to the comfort zone when what they try doesn't work. Only that small percentage, five or ten percent, will continually improve themselves; they will continually push themselves out into the zone of discomfort, and these are always the highest performers in every field." We must make a commitment with ourselves to do all that it takes to overcome our fears, eliminate our limiting belief and break our bad habits to get the success that peak performers achieve.

Thomas Edison once quoted this: *"We shall have no better conditions in the future if we*

The **ACHIEVER** Effect

are satisfied with all those which we have at present." There are four things that make us feel comfortable:

- Familiarity with location
- Familiarity with people
- Familiarity in thoughts
- Familiarity in actions

But if we cling to familiarity in these aspects of our lives, there's no opportunity for real growth — personally, professionally, or financially.

My navy experience dealt with location and people, but the changes we make in our actions can have an ever greater effect, and are key to financial gain. Working in the corporate world, anyone could grow accustomed to daily, weekly, or monthly patterns of tasks and responsibilities. Being adept or even excelling in these responsibilities isn't enough for someone who wants to make an impression and increase the possibility of being rewarded.

Here are a few ways someone could break out of the comfort zone at work:

The **ACHIEVER** Effect

- If you don't typically speak in front of others, prepare a short presentation about one of your responsibilities and share it at a meeting with your team.
- Develop a unique process improvement that has the possibility of increasing productivity, income, or whatever is important to your workgroup.
- Eagerly attempt a challenging assignment that normally would be handled by your supervisor or a "higher level."

Not everyone is wired for corporate life. In fact, corporations are full of people who aren't. They may be dreaming of some activity they would rather be doing only if money weren't a consideration.

Two former vice presidents from a company my closest friend used to work for were tired of corporate life, so they gave up their six-figure salaries to open a bed and breakfast in the Hamptons. This is happening everywhere; people are making major changes to their lives to fulfill a calling, a dream, or a passion. These changes always require a rejection of some level of comfort in pursuit of a new environment offering a possibility of self-improvement.

Aside from a career path or entrepreneurial dream, it's easy to fall into a Comfort Zone with our finances. It's easy to pay someone else to do basic yard work, for example. And if outsourcing this work is embedded in your family culture, paying someone else is natural and comfortable. There may be good reasons to outsource but in many cases there aren't, and those reasons — no time, no skill — are often excuses. Even having never picked up a rake or planted a flower, a new self-responsible gardener could save a significant amount of money over time, amplified by compound interest.

Many people avoid investing because it seems difficult or risky from the outside. How do you know which stocks to pick? How do you handle a stock market crash? Whom can you trust? With these questions, many people stick to what they're comfortable with: investing in their company's 401(k) because someone else has made the decision for them, and saving anything else they have left after expenses at the end of the month in a bank account.

The **ACHIEVER** Effect

This is the result of financial comfort. While it feels good, and this person may have a sense of security that nothing bad can happen, the opportunity cost could be significant. By *not taking action*, the would-be investor is likely losing out on thousands, tens of thousands, or perhaps even hundreds of thousands of dollars over a lifetime. This could be solved by stepping outside the comfort zone and learning how to do something new: invest.

Whether you want to be rewarded at your job, be successful on your own, improve your financial situation, or just feel like you accomplished something, the key is to break out of your comfort zone. **Even if what you are doing works for you, a little effort to try something new could result in a better outcome.** If you keep doing only what's ordinary, your results will continue to be just as ordinary. The only solution is to start doing something extra-ordinary.

But just like any move against human nature, this doesn't come naturally. So to summarize this chapter, let's go back over ways you can break out of your comfort zone:

The **ACHIEVER** Effect

- **Educate yourself.** Find out how other people achieve what *you* want to achieve with a high level of success. Research your tasks as much as possible, reading case studies, books, and blogs. Find guides that provide step-by-step instructions for the task outside your comfort zone that you wish to accomplish. Keep coming back to your resources throughout the entire process.
- **Team up.** The internet is your friend, but nothing beats spending some time in personal conversation with someone whose path you'd like to emulate. If your goal is to stop buying dinner out and start cooking every day, reading recipes will only get you so far. Have an expert help you by giving you hands-on experience under the watchful eye of a personal guide. For whatever you want to achieve, find a class that lets you participate while working with classmates, most of whom could be in the same situation as you. There is safety and comfort in numbers.
- **Create a plan.** Writing down a challenge, whether just in a notebook kept in your night stand or on a blog

public to the world, makes it real. I believe the more public, the better. (At Consumerism Commentary, I make my finances public, which means I'm accountable to the world, not just myself. This brings extra pressure, but motivation as well.) While writing, break your goal into at least three measurable accomplishments, and break those accomplishments into at least three tasks. This is your roadmap. For example, running a 5K is outside the comfort zone of many couch potatoes. In this case, a plan has been created for you. All you have to do is follow it.

- **Take small steps.** Like the first step of a couch potato on the way to her first 5K, the first step is always the most difficult. Any task that seems daunting can be broken down into smaller steps. Eventually, your series of small steps becomes your path to the goal. Some people can make the change they want in one leap once they decide to tackle the obstacle, but that's not the right choice for everyone. In general, small steps result in success because a slow

process helps to reinforce and internalize the experience — building gradual comfort.
- **Breed a *new* comfort.** As make slow progress through a series of tasks or through repetition, you're actually *expanding* your Comfort Zone. That which you never would have considered doing is now something you might do without a second thought. You may find yourself looking for more and ready to make some new plans once comfort sets in. Despite my nervousness about college, it didn't take long to feel comfortable there. I was soon looking for more challenges, such as running student organizations.

By breaking out of your comfort zone, you're opening your mind to new experiences, so it's natural for your goals and desires to change along the way. An investing newbie whose goal was to familiarize herself with the stock market may have such a great experience after the first comfort zone breach that she may be inspired to become a financial planner and to help others achieve their financial goals. The factory worker who quits his job to run his

The **ACHIEVER** Effect

own business may achieve personal success which inspires him to meet new people including his future wife.

The rewards for escaping your comfort zone are limitless. The rewards for never expanding your experience are well-defined: more of the same.

CHAPTER SIXTEEN

Faith in Your Dream

Faith is a powerful weapon in your arsenal when it comes to becoming massively successful. It is the driving force behind your passion and it is also the force that will make all things possible. Another word for faith is belief. Whatever endeavor you find yourself getting into, you must have faith. As far as creating the lifestyle that you wish, developing this faculty in your mind can be an important tool for you and your progress. If you didn't have faith or believe that the floor would support you in the morning when you got out of bed, you wouldn't take that

The **ACHIEVER** Effect

step would you? I'm talking about you really have NO faith that the floor will be there or think it will just drop you into this never ending hole or something toward that nature.

Normally, when someone starts a new business and have no faith that it will flourish, they tend to quit or give up quickly because the passionate energy to get back up after failure never arrives. If you have a dream that you would like to accomplish someday, you must believe that you will reach that destination. Just as thought controls your actions, faith can control your feelings toward your actions. More than likely, you would not act on your dream if you have no faith that it will play out the way you want it to. But perhaps we are moving too fast. In order for you to have a faith in anything else, you must start with having faith within yourself. All too often the reason why a person doesn't act on anything that they desire is because of the lack of faith in oneself. It's just like if a shy guy saw a girl he really liked but never approaches her due to fear of rejection or lack of faith within himself. He doesn't "see" himself ever scoring with a hot girl like her. So what does he do? He doesn't act at all. And without realizing it until it is too late, he gave up his chances of ever being with her when he sees another guy take the opportunity that he wasted. Not believing in yourself can definitely "steal" opportunities for you. Especially if your goal is to make more income. But fear not readers! Helping you overcome this challenge is the point to this chapter. By the time you finish reading this book, you will have the faith and all the tools you will need to master your own life and take everything to the next level.

Now let us look at some points and tips that will help you find that "inner" faith that you will need in order to move on to creating the type of lifestyle that you always wanted to live. These are only suggestions and you do not have to follow them. However, if you want to see some drastic change in your life, it is highly recommended that you follow these instructions to the letter. The goal to this is to eventually help you overcome the obstacles that may be stopping you from getting to that dream that you always wanted.

- **Set Goals-** When you set goals for yourself, you are taking control of what your next action will be.
- **Recognize when you achieve your goals-** Something as simple as this

will build your confidence as you go along on the path to your success.
- **Consider reasons you fail-** Not one person who has ever achieved their goals never failed at some point. Take those failures as lessons to build upon your character and learn from them. This way, you are now better and you will be able to achieve the goal you failed once before.
- **Use realistic expectations to judge your success-** Do not expect to run a four minute mile, until you have trained and conditioned to run a four minute mile. You can judge your success by looking at the gap between where you are and where you want to be. This perspective helps you gauge what remains to be done. You can also judge by looking at the progress you've made from 2-3 years ago or 2 months ago. This will help you figure out how far you have come. Both perspectives are valid.
- **Give your time and energy to others-** When you perform this action, you will get positive feedback and respect from others. These are building blocks for self-

respect...which is an essential step to believing in yourself.
- **Take criticism. But never allow them to convince you that you are less than what you are-** There is nothing wrong with having an open mind and accepting criticism. Use that info to build upon yourself to be the very best you that you can possibly be. This is important if making more income is your goal. If you are starting or already own a business, constructive criticism is the way to go. This way, you will meet the needs and wants of the people and create a healthier and happier relationship between you and your clients.
- **Don't give up on your dreams, goals or aspirations for you never know how right they truly are until you put them into action-** This goes back into stepping outside of your comfort zone. By never giving up on your goals, you are building more self-confidence within yourself and therefore creating a habit of successful traits.

The **ACHIEVER** Effect

With faith building up within you, you are generating a "vibration" that is being sent out into the reality of life. With that kind of power, you are unconsciously bending your circumstances to your will. You will notice that things are starting to change for you. And this isn't in any kind of pace. Things will change for you in such a drastic and amazing speed, you won't even believe that it was possible. Faith is a powerful tool to change your life completely around. Now, here is the ugly truth behind having faith in yourself. Not everybody is going to have faith or believe in you. The truth be told, it's hard the keep that faith when others around you don't. Don't allow this to hinder your progress into greatness. Also within this chapter, I will show you a program which has twelve necessary steps you must take in order to survive the "hate" that you may be feeling from others while you are on your journey to massive success. Each of these steps will help you on a day to day basis. Some may doubt you and your dream. This is a normal situation. This factor has stopped many people from doing more or becoming more because they allow others to have that kind of power and influence in their lives. Here are the twelve steps to helping one overcome this obstacle:

The **ACHIEVER** Effect

- **Try to be better than yourself**
- **Take time to play**
- **Always be the first rate version of yourself**
- **Always dream and shoot higher than you thought possible**
- **Don't bother just to be better than your predecessors**
- **Ask for what you want**
- **Laugh often**
- **Live loudly**
- **Be avid**
- **Never stop the attempt to grow. Learn new things**
- **Focus on your goals**
- **Most importantly- *BE YOURSELF***

In many cases, our great and historical figures who gained massive riches and wealth went through their own "trial of faith" when they were on the path to accomplishing their dream. The invention of the first manned aircraft in flight by the Wright Brothers is a great example of two brothers who had faith in their invention and pushed forward with unshakable conviction. *These two brothers spent a great deal of time observing birds in flight. They noticed that birds soared into the wind and that the air*

The **ACHIEVER** Effect

flowing over the curved surface of their wings created lift. Birds change the shape of their wings to turn and maneuver. The Wrights believed that they could use this technique to obtain roll control by warping, or changing the shape, of a portion of the wing. This sparked an idea within the two inventors.

Over the next three years, Wilbur and his brother Orville would design a series of gliders which would be flown in both unmanned and piloted flights. Over the course of these few years, they had a few failed attempts. But just like achieving any dream, you must pay your dues before you hit the payload! But even through those failures, they believed that they can make this work, and eventually they did! Following a successful glider test, the Wrights built and tested a full size glider. They selected Kitty Hawk, North Carolina as their test site because of its wind, sand, hilly terrain and remote location. In 1900, the Wrights successfully tested their new 50-pound glider with its 17-foot wingspan and wing-warping mechanism at Kitty Hawk, in both unmanned flights and the first piloted flight. Based upon the results of the test flights, the Wright Brothers planned to refine the controls and landing gear on the aircraft and build a bigger glider.

Now with changes comes a different set of problems that may occur. The glider was even heavier this time around with a 22-foot wingspan and the weight of nearly 100 pounds! There wasn't enough lifting power, the forward elevator was not effective in controlling the pitch, and the wing warping mechanism caused the airplane to spin out of control. The Wrights predicted in their disappointment that man will probably not fly within their lifetime. In spite of the problems they had on their last attempts at flight, the Wrights reviewed their test results and determined that the calculations they had used were not reliable. So through instant insight, they decided to build a wind tunnel to test a variety of wing shapes and their effect on lift. After a few more attempts, the Wright Brothers made history and the Vin Fiz was born. In 1911, it was the first airplane to cross the United States. The flight took 84 days, stopping at least 70 times throughout. But it eventually made it to California.

Faith in your goals and dreams can and will take you far to making them a reality. And loving what you do while you are on your

The **ACHIEVER** Effect

journey to fulfilling your life's purpose, will indeed help you get past the hard times. Few people realize that believing in yourself and having faith in your dream can indeed change your life in multitudes. Always remember these words or write it down some where you can read it every day to remind you on how you can attain your dream. *"Faith makes all things possible. Love makes all things easy."* Keep your faith alive and burning and you will redeem the benefits that await you at the end of the line.

CHAPTER SEVENTEEN

Creating the Habit

How do the rich keep getting richer and the poor keep getting poorer? Most would say that the rich are people who have all the good luck and the poor has all the bad luck. Well, allow me to shed light on your world and ensure you that isn't the case in this matter. It all boils down to habit. Having a healthy habit can not only put money in your pockets and keep it there, but it can also help improve your life tenfold. The problem that

The **ACHIEVER** Effect

exists today is that most people don't know how to go about creating a healthy habit to make more money or to improve their life. Habits have a nasty way of keep you down as well. This chapter is dedicated to showing you what effects that positive and negative habits have your life and how to go about changing a habit that may be holding you back.

Believe it or not, habits are created from the majority of our thoughts. So if the majority of your thoughts are negative, nine times out of ten your habits will reflect. Many people don't realize or choose not to see that habits controls their actions. Some people simply don't want to give up certain habits that may be hindering their progress just because they might enjoy them or it might bring them temporary comfort. But heed this warning, if your goal is to make more income and live a life of full abundance, which is the reason most people read this book, break out of your bad habits and inhabit some new and positive habits. In the course of this chapter, I will provide everyone the key to which you can start to accumulate millions of dollars and change your life drastically as quickly as you would like. But just like everything else in life, it will take much practice and dedicated effort in order to change your habits into a money making habit.

To change your habit, one must change their entire mindset. In order to become a millionaire, you must think like one. This task may be hard for some to accomplish simply because of the situation each person may be in. I can ensure you, however, this is entirely possible. Try thinking on a level that will change your persona. A lot of folks would ask, "so you are telling me to think like a snob?" The answer to that would be a no. You don't have to think like a snob. But what I am telling you is that in order to have more, you must become more than what you are right now. Simply put, what you have been doing so far hasn't been working, so it is time to try something new. This goes to changing the vibration of your thought. Remember in previous chapters that by changing your vibration of thought, you are changing how things are working for you in life. Your thoughts control your actions. So if you think like a millionaire, you will move like one as well. You will find yourself creating habits that will make you an abundance of money. This doesn't only apply to making money. You can change the vibration of thought into anything that you

The **ACHIEVER** Effect

wish. The end result will be the changing of habits which will result in attaining your goal faster. But this change must be desirable. You cannot "fake the funk" when it comes to changing your habit. Your mind will know if you mean or not. And without that "want" to change, you won't see the results that you desire. So with that being said, you must mix this with emotion.

If you feel as though you will change, and you believe it will all your heart, then you will see the results that you want. This is the time when the mind and the heart must agree to meet a common goal. One great habit of having is being decisive. Fortune does not favor the indecisive soul. When you constantly procrastinate everything, you are only delaying your fortune, your success from finding you. This horrible habit will lead you down a road of certain destruction. So it is vital that you learn how to be decisive in everything that you do. If you don't be decisive, someone else will decide for you what you future holds. That power shouldn't belong to anybody but you. Here are a few simple habits that you can look into that will most definitely put you on the fast track to wealth.

The **ACHIEVER** Effect

- **Set Big Goals-** No matter what the word rich means to you, you have to set the goal of getting there. There is nothing wrong with small goals, but to get rich you have to think big. For example, set the goal of building your wealth up to $125,000 within the next five years. If you don't want to focus solely on income, set goals based around other financial details such as paying off your mortgage in a short period of time or saving enough money to pay for large purchases with cash to avoid going into debt. Make sure while your goals should be "big" they should still be attainable. You want to challenge yourself, but don't challenge yourself with an unrealistic goal; otherwise, you will become deflated and feel let down when you don't reach those goals. Take advantage of positive reinforcement.

- **Don't lose sight of your goals-** Anybody can set a goal, but most people never do what it takes to reach them. If you want to get rich, you have to stay on the right path, no matter what gets in your way. Day after day, review your goal and make sure you are taking steps towards reaching it. Post your goals on your refrigerator, on your bathroom mirror, night stand. Stay motivated! Have somebody alongside for support. This can be anybody from a friend who is trying to accomplish a similar goal, or a spouse who is willing to work with you to make this happen. Goals are always easier to reach when you have help.

- **Keep a journal.** Not only is this is a great way to track goals and the progress that you are making, but it also gives you a place to record your feelings on money and related details. You may be surprised at how much progress you make when you begin to put your thoughts down on paper. If you get in this habit, it is easy to look back at any time and see how far you came and whether or not you are really on your way to becoming rich.

A few simple habits such as these will help you along the road to becoming successful in any endeavor you may take on. Another creative habit would be to make your own personal contract with yourself. I've noticed

The **ACHIEVER** Effect

that this will help you keep focused on your goal. Make a statement such as, "I will become a successful and well known millionaire by the end of the year". Then you would sign your name and date it right after your statement. Note that your statement can be anything you desire. As long as you put your faith behind it, this statement will have more power to it and will become a way of life for you. At least within that year you made the promise. And don't worry if you don't make the deadline. If you wind up going past it, just simply set up another deadline. This is only to remind and motivate you to keep going.

Now we get into what I like to call positive affirmations. These are powerful statements that you can make to yourself on a daily basis. Affirmations can be transformed into your actual thoughts if said frequently enough. Many times over, people use negative affirmations within their minds or said aloud to themselves. This alone can and will keep a person who wants to rise to the class of the wealthy in the poverty level. You want nothing but positive affirmations in your mind. By repeating positive affirmations daily, you are changing the vibrations of your thoughts. Remember, what you always think

The **ACHIEVER** Effect

about, you attract into your life. So it would be beneficial to you to leave the phrase "I CAN'T" out of your affirmations and your thoughts. Replace that with "I CAN". Positive reinforcement is ten times more powerful than negative and a sure way to getting exactly what you desire versus what you don't desire. If making more money is your goal, there are 3 powerful affirmations I say to myself every day and it works its magic. By saying and believing in these phrases, you are actively ensuring your success.

-*"I would love to have more money"*……..

Notice that this affirmation does not contradict a belief that you don't have enough money. Instead, simply saying "I would love" helps you focus on an easier state of being and a state of having plenty of money.

It's important to focus on the positive emotion rather than the negative emotion. You don't want to hold an attitude that reflects wanting to have more money but feeling frustrated that you don't. Instead, you want to hold an attitude that focuses on how **amazing** it would feel to have more money.

The **ACHIEVER** Effect

Can you feel the difference between the two mind-sets? When you say, "I would love to have more money," focus on the reasons why you would love to have more money. *How would it help you to have more money? What wonderful things would you do if you had more money?* Focus on those positive aspects of having more money, and within a few minutes you'll feel a positive shift happening.

-*"Money can be used for such wonderful purposes"*............

This money affirmation can help you to overcome negative beliefs such as, "Money is evil; having money is wrong; rich people are greedy people who tricked others to have their wealth," and so on. When you say, "Money can be used for such wonderful things," you start seeing money as a **tool** for goodness. Certainly it can be used in negative ways too, but when you keep reminding yourself that it can be used for positive endeavors, you lessen your resistance to allowing more money to flow into your life.

As you say this affirmation, be sure to focus on the good things you would do if you had a

The **ACHIEVER** Effect

lot of money. "Money can be used for such wonderful things." *What kind of wonderful things? How would you use your money to benefit the world; to benefit your family; to benefit yourself?*

"There are endless ways that I can receive more money"…………..

This money affirmation helps you change the limiting belief that money can only come to you through your job or other limited avenues. When you say, "There are endless ways I can receive more money," you send out an intention to the universe that you are open to receiving money through endless gateways!

You are essentially creating a new belief that the universe will then act upon. Money will start coming to you in fun and unexpected ways, which will further strengthen your belief, which will attract still more money to you! The key with this belief is to say it like you mean it. Say it with passion and power in your voice. Really do your best to ***believe*** it, even if you don't actually believe it at first. In time you will, and your outer circumstances will reflect the strength of your belief.

For best results, say at least **ONE** of these three affirmations daily. If you can, say all three of them daily, but if that's too overwhelming you can choose just one to start with. Say this affirmation not just once or twice a day - really pour your full effort into saying it over and over all day long. Say it while you are showering, while you are driving, while you are walking, shopping, watching television. You want to really saturate your mind with the ideas and start planting the seeds to form positive new beliefs about money.

Affirmations can be helpful in attracting more money and other forms of abundance into your life, but you have to choose your money affirmations carefully and use them in the most effective way. Contrary to popular belief, affirmations do not have any magical powers all on their own. The true power of an affirmation is that it improves your feelings on a particular subject. Why is this powerful?

Because the Law of Attraction is activated according to your dominant thoughts, feelings, and beliefs. So, if your thoughts are very often focused on money and abundance in negative ways, you probably think things like this often: *"I hate not having enough money. I hate being broke. It stinks that other people have more money than I do. I hate struggling to pay my bills. I hate feeling so anxious and worried all the time."* And of course, the more you think thoughts like that, the worse you feel.

When you use money affirmations to start shifting your dominant thoughts, feelings, and beliefs, you start shifting your focus in a more positive direction. However, you can't just leap from a negative state to a positive state. All you need to do is transition gradually. For this reason, your money affirmations should be worded in such a way that they help you make that shift easily and gently. If you choose money affirmations that are unbelievable, your subconscious mind will resist them and you will see not results.

For example, if you said the affirmation, *"I am wealthy"* but you aren't wealthy at the moment, your subconscious mind will block it because you know it's not true. Even worse, if you are really struggling financially, saying "I am wealthy" may stir up all kinds of negative feelings like anger, bitterness, anxiety, and resentment - which just keeps you locked in a negative state of manifestation!

The trick I am about to unveil to you came from a book written by *Napoleon Hill* called *Think and Grow Rich*. This statement has undoubtedly helped me reach levels of success one can only dream about. And I know this will help you as well. When you want to achieve something specific and you want a lot of income for doing it, it would help if you state aloud the following:

The desired amount of money I would like to receive over time is_____

And in exchange for the desired amount of _____ I will provide_____

I fully attend to have the desired amount_____
by_____

By repeating this everyday upon arising and before laying your head down to rest for the night, you are setting into motion a chain of events that may and will happen If you

The **ACHIEVER** Effect

follow the instructions, you will find yourself moving and doing things that will help you reach your goal. But as many times said before, you must put you FAITH and your HEART into. This is the only way that this trick will work for you.

CHAPTER EIGHTEEN

Time: A Wasted Factor

Life is nothing more than time you spend on this earth. It is our most precious commodity and unfortunately for a lot of people, the most wasted. A lot of people in our world today spend a lot of time watching television, talking on the phone, reading up on what is happening in celebrities' lives and so on. Doing these thing will not only stop you from living life, but will kill any hope of you fulfilling your true potential. For those looking to succeed, you must put in the time

The **ACHIEVER** Effect

and effort. Without using your time correctly, you are running out of that essential time needed to make your dream a reality. I can tell you this, you won't reach it watching television all day. With walking the path to success may come great sacrifice. There may be some things you enjoy doing now that you may have to put off until you have reached that goal you wanted to achieve.

For many us, we enjoy going out to clubs, parties, etc. But is this taking up time that you could be using to getting closer to your dream? Is this a distraction to your income? The answer to these questions would definitely be a *yes*. It is known that many people wasted their younger years partying instead of moving forward to making their dream income. Therefore, wasting the precious time that they will never get back. Time is money. This is a simple saying, but true none the less. Each minute that goes by is another dollar one could have earned. If you want to be successful, you must prioritize what is truly important to you. Is partying every weekend now helping you to

The **ACHIEVER** Effect

get closer to your goals of attaining massive success? It is way more fruitful to put in the time now and party later when you have succeeded in your goals of making more income. There is a feeling of peace of mind when you go out at that point.

Another waste of your time is watching television the entire day. There is an entire life out there waiting for you to take hold of. If you invest your time in doing nothing but watching the tube now, expect nothing later on. Many people complain about how they wish they can make more money and be wealthy like the top 1%. But they do nothing more than that. They go home and watch reality shows of billionaires and the wealthy. As they are watching, wishing that they can live the life of a superstar. This simply won't do if you plan on achieving anything. Your situation today was based off of decisions you made yesterday. If your decision is to wait for something miraculous to happen to you, you will always be in that state of waiting. It won't come for you I promise. You won't meet your goals by doing that.

The **ACHIEVER** Effect

You must put in some of the work if you want to meet your success in the middle. Success is attracted to those who are hungry for it. Success is also granted to those who invest the time into it as well. In other words, success is not bought with money, but with your time. This goes into that phrase, "you reap what you sew". The seeds you lay down today will grow with the time you put into it. Later on down the line, those seeds have grown into massive success. If you take care of those "seeds" properly. Time management is crucial to your success and should be taken very seriously. So it would help if you knew how to manage your time correctly. Well you are in luck! In the following example of 30 tips you can use in which to manage your time better. However, these are only suggestions. But if you want to be truly successful, it would be wise to take heed.

1. Make a to-do list (electronic or paper). Put the most important item first and work down from there.

The **ACHIEVER** Effect

2. At the end of your day, review what you've done and make a new list for the next day. In order of importance.

3. Be ruthless about setting priorities. Make sure that what you think is important is really important.

4. Learn to differentiate between the important and the urgent. What's important is not always urgent. What's urgent is not always important.

5. Carry your to-do list with you at all times.

6. All things being equal, do the hardest, least fun thing first. Just get it over with!

7. If a task takes less than five minutes, do it right away. If it takes longer, put it on the list.

8. Deal with E-mail at set times each day, if possible. If you need to check messages as they arrive, limit your sessions to less than five minutes.

9. Schedule some uninterrupted time each day when you can concentrate on important tasks, even if you have to take refuge in a conference room or at the library.

10. Another approach: Before you check your E-mail or voicemail or get involved in the

minutiae of the day, devote a solid hour to your most important project.

11. For a couple of days, take an inventory of how you spend your time to find out where and how you're wasting it.

12. Eliminate the time wasters (e.g., if personal phone calls are taking up too much space in your workday, turn off your cell).

13. Cut big jobs into small chunks. Order the chunks by importance. Work on one chunk at a time.

14. For big, complex tasks, schedule wiggle room. Projects tend to take longer than you think/hope. Give yourself a buffer.

15. If part of your day involves routine repetitive tasks, keep records of how long they take and then try to do them faster.

16. Go one step further and set specific time limits for routine tasks. Work tends to fill whatever amount of time you happen to have.

17. Establish smart efficient systems for all your tasks, big and small, and stick to them.

18. Value your time. People who wander into your workspace to chat do not respect you or your schedule. Set boundaries.

The **ACHIEVER** Effect

19. When and where you can, say no. Trying to do everything everyone asks you to do is a recipe for failure.

20. In general, guard against over scheduling yourself.

21. Bottom line to items 19 and 20: Learn to delegate, wherever and whenever you can.

22. Aim to handle pieces of paper only once. Same for E-mails. Read them and deal with them.

23. Reward yourself for completing tasks on time. No fun stuff until the work stuff is done.

24. Organize your workspace so you don't waste time looking for things.

25. Schedule demanding tasks for that part of your day when you're at your peak.

26. Group related tasks (e.g., sort papers on your desk and then file them). It's more efficient.

27. Use down time (e.g., waiting for meetings to begin) to, for example, update your to-do list or answer E-mails.

The **ACHIEVER** Effect

28. This advice applies to life outside work, too. It's better to be excellent at a few things than average at many.

29. Don't be afraid to get projects done early. It takes them off your mind, and it doesn't mean you'll just be given more to do.

30. Create the business environment that works for you. Adjust the lighting, turn off your E-mail notifications, and get that cup of tea. Set the stage and get to work.

CHAPTER NINETEEN

Plan on the Mastermind

The most amazing thing about the human race is that we are capable of doing anything once we put our minds together. Your path to success will be filled with many potholes and quick turns. So it would be best if you took a group with you! The fact of the matter is, we

The **ACHIEVER** Effect

can't do it by ourselves. The best and quickest way to achieving your goals is to have a "mastermind" group behind you for support. There may be some areas that we may require help on. It would be great if we were experts on everything. But the truth is, we're not perfect. Assembling a "mastermind" group will not only improve your chances for making it to your final destination earlier, but you will make it there whole and intact. It's great to have people that are strong in areas that you may not be so strong at. This should be your first stage of planning whenever you decide on what you want to do.

Many companies that are up and running successfully now started off with a small group of individuals who all shared a similar dream. It is foolhardy to believe that you will make it on your own. So make this a priority when you are first starting out. Even King Author of legend has his round table with his queen, his wizard Merlin, and his most trusted knights. Within this story, we learn that King Author did not run the

The **ACHIEVER** Effect

kingdom a Camelot by himself. He often sought counsel from his group when it came to matters of the kingdom. So basically, you will need help in order to build your empire. Within the "mastermind" group you will learn how to:

¨ Interface with intelligent, forward moving people

¨ Have a safe environment for sharing ideas

¨ Have other minds focused for a period of time on your specific innovative ideas or challenges

¨ Have a shortened learning curve when engaged in new ventures

¨ Gain specialized knowledge

¨ Gain inspiration

¨ Benefit from the experience and wisdom of the group

¨ Contribute your own specialized knowledge to others

The **ACHIEVER** Effect

" Overcome anxiety

" Expand your abilities

" Empower yourself for success.

Your mastermind group should have no more than six members. It your group winds up being too small, you lose dynamics and diversity of ideas. However, watch it if it gets too big. This can cause the group meetings to last a whole lot longer. Which isn't necessarily all that bad. But people might have pressing matters to attend to in their own personal lives.

Having this type of group can help you draw up a blueprint to your course of action that needs to be taken in order to achieve the attended goal. There has been many businesses out there that didn't start with this group and failed because they didn't have the skills in every area to prosper. Once again, and I must stress this point, you must find people who have the same goal in mind as you do or the group will fall apart due to differences of opinion. In this group, you must all move as one mind. So be careful at choosing your people. Your group should also meet at least two times a week to discuss new ideas and concepts that could take everyone's progress to the next level. These meetings should be no longer than 1 to 2 hours each time. Make sure to write down each new idea and concept that may have been mentioned in the meeting. You may need more time to mow over each idea and see where it can fit into your plan. Remember, planning is like putting together a puzzle board. It takes time but eventually you will see the entire picture.

It is truly a wonderful feeling when you are surrounded with likeminded individuals who all want the same outcome as you do. This will push your progress even faster. We as humans, were always meant to work together to reach a common goal. Two minds or more is definitely better than one in this case. Planning is essential for you to attain the master key of success. Without it, you are left will nothing but failed attempts and you

The **ACHIEVER** Effect

might not ever see your plans come to fruition. So best you be prepared for anything!!!

CHAPTER TWENTY

Standing Out and Being Seen

A person who stands out from the crowd is someone who is comfortable with who they are, has the confidence to be unique and to let their individuality shine. Standing out from the crowd means that you're not afraid to speak your mind and to avoid following others when to do so results in sameness and conformity. A person who stands out from the crowd may be someone whose

The **ACHIEVER** Effect

appearance is striking in some way, but more often than not, it is about someone who generates admiration and is remembered by others for being someone special and worthy of looking up to.

While standing out from the crowd might not be something you can achieve every day of your life, it's definitely a worthwhile goal to aspire to as a whole, especially if it helps you achieve your other goals in life. We were all meant to shine as children do. Many people would say that only the certain people has the "luck" to be discovered and made into a superstar. But if you look even closer, chances are they were picked up because they stood out from the rest of the crowd. Standing out in a positive way can do wonders for you within your life, on your dream job, or in the business world. By you going after your dreams and doing what you wish to do in this life, you are already standing out from the majority of people today. You have the courage to risk it all to ensure that you meet your "destiny" head on! That alone makes you special. But everybody can be special in their own way. Just need to find that inner courage.

It all begins when you decide what standing out from the crowd means for you. Is this about looking as different from everyone else around you as you can possibly be or is it about going the extra mile to prove that you are one of a kind in skills, talent, or personality? Standing out from the crowd might be about trying to live your best and be your best. Or, it might be about trying to have a unique style or look that you've created yourself without borrowing from other people's ideas. At its most basic, standing out from the crowd means embracing your individuality and trusting that your own choices are good ones. The person you're projecting out to everyone will stand out more successfully if you're fully confident about yourself.

Stepping out from the crowd also means that you can think for yourself. Standing out from the crowd won't happen if you're thinking with the crowd. While there will be times when the crowd-think does align with

The **ACHIEVER** Effect

your own thoughts, what about all those times it hasn't? Be prepared to voice your differences, your concerns, and your preferences. When talking, it is important to come across as self-assured and knowledgeable, so be sure to have done your research and know your facts beforehand.

Try not to be swayed by the crowd. The pace of the crowd can be relentless and the ease with which the crowd can change its mind, its clothes, or its latest fad is breathtaking. Barely anyone in the crowd stops a moment to wonder if this shared momentum is responsible in a big picture way or whether it's conscious of individual needs. If you want to stand out from the crowd, you're going to need to stop and ask the hard questions, such as "Is there a point to this?" or "Just because everyone else has X gadget, why do I also need one? Will it enhance my life?"

Take chances or risks, invest your time, and work hard. Risks and chances are the things in life that can catapult you forward if they work out. Many people won't take up the challenge because they're afraid of failure.

The **ACHIEVER** Effect

Yet, without failure nothing new can be gained and it is only those who are willing to take risks and to work hard at their dreams that eventually break through and succeed. Have a well-placed sense of faith in your mission, and a willingness to take risks if you want to stand out from the crowd.

Try to do things differently. Find new ways to get people's attention and to stay noticed. Many people have found out how to create jobs and/or high profiles for themselves by using the internet in amazing ways, such as blogs, gimmicks, videos, and more. For example, Kyle Clarke created an online campaign called "Hire Me" in which he encouraged employers to bid for him and he ended up with more job offers than he knew what to do with in a time of recession. And Alex Tew invented the Million Dollar Homepage to raise money for his university education, a website in which he sold one million pixels, grossing him over one million dollars and spawning many copycats. And of course there are sites like Facebook and

The **ACHIEVER** Effect

Twitter, demonstrating the power of being the first to do things differently and to stand out from the crowd. These kinds of unique initiatives are bound to make you stand out from the crowd; you'll just need to be the first to do something differently.

One thing my grandmother told me years ago and it always stuck with me was that manners will places money never will. And it does! Actually, manners will definitely help out in that area. *Politeness opens doors and keeps them open. Manners might seem old-fashioned to some these days but they are the currency of respect and when a person feels respected, they remember the well-mannered person forever. People are very fond of telling one another about the rare acquaintance of theirs who has "impeccable manners"; make sure that person is you.*

It's the little things that count. Little things such as:

- *Say thank you for all the little things people do, as well as the big things. Send thank you cards to people who have helped you with a deadline, held open a door for you when your hands were full, or took you out for a lovely evening. In business this is also very important when people you've networked with help you on your way.*

- *Shake people's hands with strength and passion. Show them from the outset that you're someone with heart and conviction.*

- *Smile. There are never enough smiles to go around; be someone who provides at least five smiles for every one frown you spot.*

Do what you say you'll do. In other words, be a man or woman of your word. When you make a promise to someone, do your very best to keep it. People who stand out from the crowd are people who keep their word and follow up their promises to help, to be somewhere, to do something for someone. The reason you'll stand out is because so

The **ACHIEVER** Effect

many people do not do what they say they will. Reliability makes you memorable and causes you to stand well above all the forgotten promise-breakers.

Show initiative. Standing out from the crowd often means that you take action while everyone else stands back, wondering what to do next. If you learn to sum up situations quickly and to respond according to what needs to be done, you place yourself in a position of being different from the silent majority waiting to be shown what should happen next.

There was a time where in history where showing initiative was the cool thing to do. Now days you may get heckled for it. Pay no attention to those who make fun of you because you showed initiative. That alone proves that you have what it take to be successful. Those who lack the initiative are not self-starters and probably will wind up working for you one day! Innovate at work, school, at home, and in your volunteer group. Be the first to point out what's working and what is not, and how to make the most of

The **ACHIEVER** Effect

what's great and improve on what's not. Leadership requires tenacity and certainty of purpose and will ensure that you stand out from the crowd. Also, if you see someone in trouble, don't assume they're getting help. Stop and ask if they need help to change the tire, or to pick up their dropped papers. Call the police if you see someone in terrible trouble and it's too dangerous to intervene; don't assume someone else has already done so!

Now, when it comes to business or you enter into an endeavor that requires a good self-image, you should take care to dress stylishly and wear what suits you. Clothing speaks in its own way, and a well-tailored outfit that fits you perfectly is bound to have people notice you. Get yourself fitted in good clothes and only buy a few of the best rather than a lot of the cheapest. Durable, perfectly-fitting clothes will free you from having to worry about your appearance because you just know you look good, whatever physical attributes you were born with. You must also ensure good grooming too. Keep your hair in fantastic shape and keep your skin and nails clean and well cared for.

Its take more than dressing good to stand out however. Make sure you check your posture. The person who stands out from the crowd will also stand tall, no matter your height. Slouching is a defensive strategy that does nothing to draw attention to you in a crowd, not to mention its harm for your overall body alignment. If you're having difficulties standing tall, talk to a physiotherapist who might be able to help you improve your posture through exercise and stretching. Usually though, it's enough to remind yourself to stand up straight, to keep your chin up, and to make eye contact with others.

One pleasantry that you can show other people of importance and it will take you a long way with them is showing your attentiveness. The greatest honor you can do another person is to show you've really heard them, and to show that what they've said matters. Since most people are too busy wondering what to say next, and how to explain their own thoughts, feelings, and ideas, a listener will stand out from the rest. Be willing to give people the space to talk about themselves and show that you clearly respect their thoughts. Not only will this flatter them and reassure them that they matter, but they'll realize very quickly that you're someone to treasure and they'll follow your lead. Put away the cell phone in restaurants, at meetings, and during conversations. Having a romantic get together? Turn the cell phone right off. Having a chat with friends? Leave the cell phone in your bag, even when it rings. Also, it would benefit you to stop your eyes from wandering around the crowd when you're with someone. Focus fully on them and be truly interested in them; this will show them that they're the one standing out from the crowd in your eyes. In turn, they'll see you as the most amazing person around.

And the final and best thing you can do to single yourself out is to remind people how great they are. Regularly single out people in your life, from the workplace to home, to remind them how great they are. So few of us take the time to acknowledge the people in our lives whom we take for granted that when someone does validate us in this way, it comes as a totally sweet surprise and is so out of the ordinary that it gets remembered. It's also a very genuine way of establishing rapport with people, and maintaining goodwill.

Walking the path to achieving your dream will be a long and winding road. But as said before, it can be as long as you make it. You will have your ups and downs. You will meet people who will greatly influence your life and people who were only meant to be an obstacle to test your character. You never know what life with throw at you next. So you best be prepared for it. Follow these guidelines that I have provided for you within the contents of this book and you will see dramatic changes in your life. Changes that you probably never thought possible. Your fate, your destiny, your purpose is what you make of it. You can have anything that you desire. It all just takes one thought to change

The **ACHIEVER** Effect

everything. Follow your bliss and watch the money follow you. Go for your target weight with unshakable conviction and watch yourself transform into a person you never thought existed. This is your universe and you are the centerpiece to it. It's your turn to be one of the greats.

"Who am I to be as so bold to believe that I can weave my name into the fabric of world history? Then again, who am I not to believe?"- Lorenzo Sellers

ABOUT THE AUTHOR

Lorenzo Sellers, was born on October 27, 1987 in a small town named Orangeburg within the state of South Carolina. He lived with his younger brother Avery Sellers, his older sister Donyelle Williams, and his mother Mary Sellers. His writing aspirations began when he was 10 years old while he lived with his now deceased grandmother, Ellen Williams who inspired him to keep writing. But his passion for it subsided after her passing. 7 years later, he joined the US Navy in hopes to finding his purpose. After 7 years of military service, Lorenzo was inspired once again to write after he realized that his passion was to help people positively change their lives after the passing of his father, Samuel Sellers. He has helped propelled many people's lives by inspiring them to unlock their hidden potential and showing them how to achieve their dreams. While still serving his country, he is now working on becoming a successful motivational speaker, success/business coach, and author. Although his main target is to help the younger generations unlock their potential before graduating high school and college, his hopes are to help companies spark up additional revenue and increase value within the companies. His dream is to one day be a international inspiration to people and change the world. He plans on writing more books in the future as he makes a name for himself as *"The Game Changer"*.

He has started his own company entitled, The Life Mastery Foundation, in hopes that it will serve as a vehicle to drive his dreams of changing the world into a reality. The Life Mastery Foundation is moving forward to helping millions of people gain a new perspective on life as they teach how one can master his or her own life and achieve any goals that they may desire. This company is dedicated to helping the majority of our youth in high schools and even college attain the mindset of success and have the lifestyle that they desire. The main objective of this company is not only to help big name companies increase their revenue, but to also help cut the struggle that happens within the transition of students from school life to the real world. Success driven, the Life Mastery Foundation WILL NOT fail at its objectives and will create a better economy for all.

www.ingramcontent.com/pod-product-compliance
Lightning Source LLC
Chambersburg PA
CBHW051801170526
45167CB00005B/1838